CHOCKS AWAY!

Woodfield Publishing Ltd

Woodfield House ~ Babsham Lane ~ Bognor Regis ~ West Sussex ~ PO21 5EL
telephone 01243 821234 ~ **e-mail** enquiries@woodfieldpublishing.com

Interesting and informative books on a variety of subjects

For full details of all our published titles, visit our website at
www.woodfieldpublishing.com

Chocks Away!

*The Memoirs and Letters
of Wing Commander*
J. Leighton Beck DFC & Bar

Woodfield

First published in 2007 by

WOODFIELD PUBLISHING
Bognor Regis, West Sussex, England
www.woodfieldpublishing.com

© John Leighton Beck, 2007

The right of John Leighton Beck
to be identified as Author of this work
has been asserted in accordance with
the Copyright, Designs and Patents Act 1988

ISBN 1-84683-038-9

Dedicated to my wife 'Budge' and my family

and to so many of my fellow officers and airmen who

lost their lives in this gigantic life and death struggle

over eleven years 1936 ~ 1946

The Author ~ India 1943.

~ CONTENTS ~

The Author, Commissioned as Pilot Officer 1936
taken at RAF Depot Uxbridge whilst on
Discipline and King's Regulations study course

Foreword

When I arrived in Jersey in January 2001, I felt very fortunate to be spending the next five years on an island with a world-wide reputation for friendliness, for generosity and for being the home of so many people with outstanding military records. Leighton Beck, even though he was not a Jerseyman by birth, characterised all those attributes and many more. My wife and I were lucky enough to meet him and his delightful wife, Budge, on a number of occasions. Needless to say, I was always fascinated to hear about his extraordinary wartime service in the Royal Air Force. By any standards, he was unquestionably an exceptional operational pilot and leader and I felt very privileged to have been in his company. It was therefore with great sadness that I learned of his death in January 2003. The more so because, having read *Chocks Away*, I did not have the opportunity to return his book to him in person.

This book is a remarkable story of one man's decade of hazardous service in almost every theatre of operations during World War II. Unlike many of his fellow bomber pilots, Leighton Beck lived to tell the tale. It is a tale that I commend to all those who are interested in the incredible and unremitting challenges that confronted our forebears when they were in their late teens and early twenties. These were challenges on a global scale that lasted throughout the seven long years of the war and beyond. Leighton Beck and his peers were indeed remarkable young men. I salute them all.

Air Chief Marshal Sir John Cheshire, KBE, CB
Former Lieutenant-Governor of Jersey

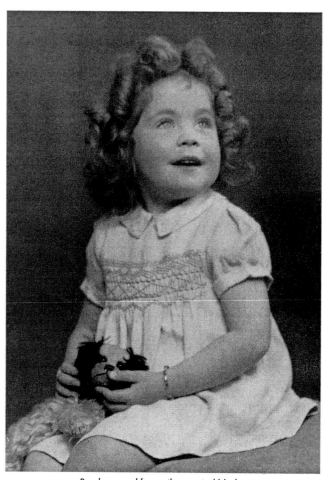

Penelope, aged four ~ the age at which she
saw her Daddy for the first time in 1944.

Preface

At the age of four (very nearly five!), holding my mother's hand, and clutching my doll 'Carol' I was on my way to meet my father for the first time. I wore a pink outfit with leggings and matching poke bonnet, as did my doll, and Mummy cut a dash in a beautifully fitted costume and matching hat.

My mother's excitement at seeing her husband after four years of wartime separation was obvious – I remember her telling me for days before that we were going to see "Daddy". The meeting place was the Savoy Hotel in the Strand, London and looking up the flight of steps to the doorway, I saw a tall man dressed in blue. I recognised the uniform from a photograph at home. Within seconds he had swooped down and clasped me to his face; an experience I did not care for because of his prickly moustache. Then he took my mother in his arms and gave her a long and passionate kiss. I had never seen anyone kiss like that before!

It was a confusing moment for a child who had relied solely on her mother's company in a remote cottage in Suffolk, and I demanded to know "where's my other Daddy?" It was an innocent question but one that might have rung alarm bells in the mind of any recently-returned husband. My mother bent gently down and asked what I meant. The explanation was simple: at home she had two photographs, each referred to as "Daddy" but in one he wore his blue RAF uniform, while in the other he was in jungle kit with a big bush hat. I had a lot to learn about having a "Daddy" and he had a lot to learn about being part of a family again.

The end of World War Two meant life was about to change for families throughout the country, and ours was no exception. My mother was a bright, sociable young woman in her early twenties who had fled with her baby from her mother's home in Bedford Park in London, after receiving a coded telegram from my father warning about "doodlebug" bombs, and entreating her to leave the Capital. She went by train to Suffolk where she set up home in a tiny cottage in Stetchworth near Newmarket. The cottage was basic, there was no bathroom, and Mummy had to fetch water from a pump in the village. Three times a week she would pay a shilling at the local pub for a bath and I would sit on the floor whilst she sang as she bathed. It was a lonely life just with a toddler for company, in a village where she was regarded as an outsider with a strange "posh" London accent.

Twice a week there was a bus into Newmarket and Mummy would visit the market to buy "Bakelite" beakers. Back home she would decorate them with painted fairies and gnomes, before taking them back to sell to a stall-holder the following week. It provided her with an interest and a little extra income. The visits to Newmarket were a diversion for me too, as the town was full of American servicemen who gave my mother wolf-whistles, and me chocolate!

So having had the full attention of my Mummy, suddenly I found I had to share her with "this Daddy"; it wasn't easy. The very first morning after we returned to Stetchworth I was told, to my fury, that I must knock on their bedroom door before bursting in. Then to cap it all "this Daddy" spread a whole week's butter on his toast; didn't he know about food rationing?

Of course we soon became accustomed to our new family life, and before too long I had a baby sister...

As I grew up it never occurred to me to talk to my father about what he did during the war. Sometimes my sister and I might ask how many Germans or Japs he killed, but we had no appreciation what people had been through and the sacrifices they made so that we could enjoy our freedom.

It was seeing the film *The Dambusters* that had the greatest effect on me, as some of the footage was from the war, and my father told me that his squadron was in the film. I began to listen to what he had to say. Like many "war children" I might never have known the part he played but for a remarkable chain of events. When he was eighty-eight my father developed a problem with his heart, which made him think he would not live for much longer. He decided to write down his wartime story which he did in long-hand. I was astonished to discover that, despite the passage of over fifty years, his memory was able to pick out some of the finer details of touch and taste.

He wrote in the style which he had been taught, and I think it should be kept that way. It is therefore authentic to the period described.

Going off to fight for King and Country may have seemed a huge adventure for many young men, but no-one could have envisaged that the separation from their loved ones would be so long. During their four years apart my mother and father wrote to one another at least once a week, despite their letters taking weeks, and often months to reach their destination. More than sixty years later these remarkable documents, which bear witness to their undying love and steadfast resolve to one day resume a normal family life, remain neatly tied in bundles of faded blue airmail paper in a battered tin box.

The early letters reflect a positive approach to going into battle, but as the war ground on, the harsh reality of its duration and nature began to replace optimism with depression. As the letters went back and forth, when one was down and miserable the other responded with hope and determination, a constant roller-coaster of emotion.

Besides these poignant outpourings the letters from my father also gave an on-the-spot account of his life, and echo, reinforce and illuminate passages from his memoirs. For this reason, (and I have to say after much heart searching) I have selected some passages from the letters he wrote to my mother for inclusion in this book.

Although my father wrote his memoirs for the benefit of his family, I feel it is of interest to a wider audience. I hope that in reading about his experiences you might have an inkling of the fears, hardships and humour shared by so many ordinary men and women, yet which so often died with them.

Penelope Avison (née Beck), July 2007

Acknowledgements

I would like to thank my dear friend Jill Hopkins, for her journalistic input in assembling the letters and memoirs. Without her enthusiasm and patience, the letters would not have been included.

With special thanks to Chris Thomas of Expressions Photography Jersey for his assistance in compiling these memoirs.

Thanks also to F.E. Wrightson & Associates for their help and advice with the IT work, and to Penny Hewson for translating the German propaganda leaflets

The Jersey Evening Post, The Daily Telegraph and *The Times* kindly gave their permission to reproduce the obituaries to Wing Commander J.L. Beck DFC & Bar, which are subject to copyright.

Penelope Avison, July 2007

The Author (right) at Elementary Flying
Training School Hanworth 1936.

Author aged 19 ~ before RAF training.

Engaged! But the struggle of War looms.

Author in flying kit in front of Blackburn B2
Trainer ~ Hanworth 1936.

1.   Pre-War ~ 1912-39

I was born in Bedford Park at No.1 Queen Anne's Grove – in London's first garden city, located between Chiswick and Acton in West London – on 15th November 1912.

I received early education at Colet Court Preparatory School in Hammersmith and adult education at Ardingly College, near Haywards Heath in Sussex.

On leaving school I had no idea of what to take up as a career. I had achieved (Oxford and Cambridge) school certificate and I was good at the usual sports provided by Public Schools of that period. An average pupil but excelling in ball games, football, cricket, track sports, etc, and was a first class shot – so much so that I was Captain of the shooting eight for two years.

I was also a keen member of the OTC. It is quite funny to recall that we wore World War One uniforms, with knee breeches and puttees and paraded with Martini rifles (and later WW1 Lee-Enfield rifles). I was also a member of the bugle and drum band and as I was rather tall I was chosen to bang away on the big drum, entitling me to wear a leopard skin apron, which was, of course, the reason I joined the band! It was in the OTC that I learned to shoot. I much enjoyed Summer Camp fortnights at Tidworth, Pirbright and other camps, on manoeuvres with the Regular Army. We were members of the Royal Sussex Regiment. I also shot at Bisley with the School Eight in the Public Schools Ashburton Competition. In my last year as Captain of the shooting eight the College won the Marling cup outright and I personally won the

Daily Telegraph sharpshooting competition. We came 6th in the Ashburton and won the "Country Life" Public Schools Trophy outright.

I was articled to a firm of Valuers, Auctioneers and Estate Agents in the City of London and Ealing Broadway, namely Ferris & Puckridge. Later I joined the firm of Debenham Tewson & Chinnocks in the City of London, a well-known Valuers Auction-eers & Estate Agents, even today. In the first firm in this profession I was detailed by my boss to collect rents, as our rent collector was on holiday, and as soon as I arrived at the door a woman grabbed my arm and rushed me into a bedroom shouting, "you've come just in time Doctor, the water has broken – hurry". I was an innocent young man, brought up in a sheltered, well-mannered home, and I left the house very red-faced. On another occasion I went with my boss to a luxury flat in Kensington, which we had let to a French lady, who complained bitterly that the bidet was too small. When we asked "how come", she pulled up her skirts, exposing a large bottom, barely concealed by frilly knickers, sat down on it and moving from side to side shrieked, "see, eet dos not feet!" More red face from yours truly!

In the spring of 1935, on a fine sunny day, my boss and I were working on the job of bringing the Ordnance Survey map up to date in an area of the Thames estuary in Leysdown, on the Isle of Sheppey in Kent. We were having a sandwich lunch on a small hill overlooking the beach eastwards towards Shellness when, in the distance, I observed a small biplane approaching from the South. It flew across the beach and out to sea. I then saw tiny white smoke puffs appearing on the surface out to sea. On closer observation I saw a round floating object that was obviously the target, surrounded by the puffs of smoke. After several runs the plane landed in a field and a tiny figure got out and walked over to a hut for a few minutes before re-appearing, taking off again and disappearing into the distance. Several similar planes repeated the exercise and by this time my interest and excitement was thoroughly aroused to such an extent that I could think of nothing else on my way home except the beauty and grace of these aeroplanes. Thus was my introduction into the wonderful world of flying.

It is a curious fact that for a number of years I had had many dreams of being able, by sheer willpower, to rise from my bed and fly around the streets of my locality in Bedford Park. Maybe these dreams of flying in my adolescent years were latent until seeing the reality of flying at the age of 22 sparked off my enthusiasm – enough to make me determined to find ways and means of learning to fly.

Shortly afterwards Sir Alan Cobham's flying circus came to Hounslow and I managed to get a five shilling trip in one of his machines and was thrilled, despite the noise of the engines and the cold wind whistling in. Later on I managed to get a ticket to see the RAF annual flying show at Hendon which also thrilled me by the enormous skill of the pilots doing acrobatics in formation, tied together wing-tip to wing-tip with bunting.

In the meantime I was engaged in taking my finals of the Chartered Surveyors exams, having taken and passed the intermediate the year before.

Handley Page Heyford at RAF Mildenahall ~ in service 1933-37.

Hawker Harts and Audaxes at No.8 FTS Montrose 1936.

2.   RAF Service ~ 1936-46

In July or August 1935 I saw an advert in a newspaper that thrilled me to the core. It gave details for young men who might be interested in joining the RAF on a short service commission in the general duties flying branch. At that time the service was expanding in a vain attempt to catch up, as it became clear that Hitler's Germany had become a real threat to peace in Europe.

I applied immediately but had to wait some months before going to the Air Ministry for an interview. It was unnerving to present oneself before a panel of middle-aged RAF officers, who asked all sorts of questions about my education and schooldays, particularly my OTC activities and especially my shooting record. This was followed by a medical, in the course of which I was spun round in a revolving chair, fast and for a fair length of time, and then was told to walk through an open doorway. This was difficult, but I managed to get through without hitting the sides (you try it and see how you get on!). A tuning fork was passed round the back of my head and I had to say when I heard it first and on which side.

I passed OK, but owing to Christmas coming up it was not until the New Year that I was told to report to Hanworth Airfield to receive initial flying training at No. 5 Elementary and Reserve Flying Training School.

All thoughts of taking my finals of the Chartered Surveyors exam went out of my head and when I told my father he was somewhat taken aback but he and mother supported me. He had been a Territorial Officer (Major) in the 1914/18 war. Although I didn't think much about it at the time, I came to realise much later how wonderful it was of them not to stand in my way. They had already lost two sons in accidents; I was their last son and they had spent a good deal of money on my education to launch me as a Surveyor and Property Agent.

Nevertheless, these things happen when one is young and I never thought about flying being dangerous at that time. Here I was being given the chance to fly the best and most advanced machines in the world and being paid to do so into the bargain!

I spent two months at Hanworth, being trained on Blackburn B2 all-metal biplanes. These were unusual in that the pupil and instructor sat side by side. The school was managed and run by Flying Training Ltd and staffed by mainly ex-RAF pilots. My instructor was Mr Wilson, known as 'Siskin Nose Wilson'. He had come to grief while on service in the RAF, his dented nose the result of tipping up one of the Siskin aircraft he used to fly when landing. After the War, he broke the flying speed record in a RAF Meteor aircraft along the South Coast.

Initial training involved pre flying checks, taking off into the wind, straight and level flying, climbing, gliding with engine off, landing and judging distances medium turns, steep turns, spinning (a hair raising experience) aerobatics – looping and rolling and practising emergency landings, side slipping. One's instructor could, at any moment, cut the engines and one had to immediately take over, put the nose down to prevent stalling, get up flying speed, look around for a suitable place to land and observe smoke from chimneys, flags or clothes on washing lines to get the wind direction for landing. Accuracy was essential, as if it was for real, one only had one chance to find a field long enough to land safely without clipping hedges or running into objects at the end of one's landing run.

After 8½ hours instruction Mr Wilson taxied to the flight hut, got out casually and just said, "OK, take off and do two or three circuits on your own." I had not expected this and my heart was racing as I taxied out into wind, did all the safety checks, especially looking to see that there was no other aircraft coming in behind, then opening up the throttle, rumbling over the bumpy turf and taking off on my first solo.

I took off smoothly enough, as I had been taught, but it was a funny, lonely feeling after getting airborne and into smooth air. As I eased back the joystick, with the familiar engine noise heard from within my leather flying helmet, I suddenly realised that I was on my own – with all the things that could go wrong if I didn't watch out. After a few minutes, with eyes glued to the instruments to check speed, height, etc, I gingerly turned to port, with slight pressure on the rudder bar and a slight side movement in co-ordination on the joystick, to bank and make a turn to port for a circuit downwind before turning crosswind for the final turn to port for the landing, making sure the plane was in the right direction into wind and at the right height over the edge of the airfield for a safe landing run.

After several similar "circuits and bumps" I could make smooth take-offs and reasonably good landings, finally taxiing to the flight hut, drenched in sweat, but happy to be congratulated by my instructor.

Our course of some 30 men was housed in a private house with large rooms used as dormitories. Most were English, Scots or Welsh, with a sprinkling of men from Canada, Australia and New Zealand. I struck up a friendship with Jobson and Macfarlane, both from New Zealand. All of us progressed to squadron level as pilot officers, but sadly both were killed in flying accidents before the outbreak of war.

It was not unknown in those days for exuberant pilots to divert on a cross-country flight to 'shoot up' their girlfriends and show off. This was generally OK if one was not seen doing so and reported, but there were too many unfortunate cases of mis-judgement of height when performing aerobatics, when the planes 'ploughed-in' out of control. Macfarlane was killed in one such incident. Given that huge sums of money were spent in the armed services on equipment and training it was understandable that the Air Ministry took a dim view of such cases and the resultant waste of public money.

After some 120 hours flying the course came to an end and those who had passed were posted to RAF Uxbridge for a discipline and lecture course. The camp had a WWI look about it. On either side of the entrance, as I recollect, there was a large bomb standing upright on its fins and painted red, white and blue. They had been produced right at the end of WWI for bombing targets deep in Germany but were never used because of the Armistice on 11th November 1918.

The barrack-type buildings were functional in appearance and parade grounds, gyms and lecture rooms abounded.

As soon as we arrived we were subjected to intense discipline. Most of the square-bashing sergeants had been formerly Army men and their voices were sharp and loud. What they said into our tender ears led us to believe that we were born out of wedlock and that they doubted we could ever be normal, disciplined service-men. Sarcasm was rife. On the whole we expected and accepted this, but by Jove we learnt the parade ground movements fast!

Those of us who had been in school OTC had an advantage, as we were used to drilling with rifles, the only difference being that at school we formed fours, as in WWI, when moving off in column, instead of in threes. I remember the weather was hot for May and 'square-bashing' was hot work.

Squadron Leader I.R. Jones, a WWI fighter ace, was our Chief Instructor. In our first lecture he said:

"Do you know what you are here for in the RAF?"

"No, Sir," was the reply, "except to learn to fly..."

"No!" he thundered. "You are here to be killed..."

We fell about laughing.

"...unless you quickly learn your discipline on the ground and in the air – particularly in the air."

At the time war seemed unlikely, so we took little notice of his opening remark, but at the back of our minds we knew that discipline would be vital if we were ever put to the test.

At the start we drilled in civilian clothes, mainly sports coats with rather baggy flannel slacks, topped overall by a pork-pie hat, usually sporting a colourful pheasant feather in the band. Before we started we were "fell in" by the Discip Sergeant and I, being tall, was in the rear rank. As soon as the squad was called to attention the sergeant called out, "Will the hofficer in the rear rank with the pretty fevver in 'is 'at, step forward and remove same. We don't want any fancy dress' ere, do we?"

To keep the peace I, of course, obliged.

Throughout our training, Warrant Officers were addressed as 'Sir' and both they and Sergeants were treated with the greatest respect. They were all hand-picked 'toughies' who really knew their jobs well and they deserved respect as they pretty well ran the show.

Later on we received our uniforms – mine from Gieves – and they made us feel we really were in the RAF. No.1 Parade uniform of blue Barathea jacket with belt and brass buttons, black tie, blue shirt, trousers and black shoes and the tight fitting blue 'monkey jacket' mess kit with gold stripes down the side of skin-tight trousers, worn with shiny gloss "Jimimas" (ankle boots with elastic sides), stiff butterfly collar, stiff white shirt front and black tie.

All this period at Hanworth and Uxbridge I was seeing Budge whenever I had the chance of a few hours off duty. My father once volunteered to drive her down to visit and I was horrified and turned the offer down straight away. He had only recently acquired the Morris Saloon car and was still learning to drive. I think he expected every other vehicle on the road to give way to him, so I wasn't taking any chances with him driving Budge. It wasn't long before he gave up driving altogether and allowed me to drive it. In those days one didn't need tuition or any permission to take a car on the roads. One was simply given a few lessons by a car owner on quiet roads until one was confident, but to re-enforce my driving skills I took one of the first RAC tests.

At the end of the 'discip' course at Uxbridge I was posted to No.8 Flying Training School at Montrose, on the east coast of Scotland, between Dundee and Aberdeen. This was a grass airfield right by the seashore and next to Montrose Golf course. It had been a WWI airfield and the old hangers were still there, although the tarmac and wooden huts which comprised the rest of the camp were new and comfortable. Our intake consisted of some 30 officers and NCOs with 100-120 hours flying in their log books. On arrival we unpacked our belongs in comfortable small rooms in huts which were well equipped as bed-sits with desks, chairs, tea service, bed, bookshelves and a small stove in one corner.

We soon settled into a routine. Early morning we marched from the mess to the flight office, accompanied by a pipe band. The skirl of the pipes is a wonderful sound and I have never lost the thrill of hearing them all through my life. Here we spent a very busy six months of advanced flying training on Hawker Harts and Audaxes, which were then in service as fighter/bombers. Their large size (to us after the small initial trainers) rather daunted us at first. A biplane, with open cockpit, they had a single, snarling Rolls-Royce Kestrel engine as their power plant. In front was the pilot, who let himself down into the open cockpit via two hand grips set in the upper wing. The observer/gunner sat behind, inside in a small compartment, with a Lewis gun mounted on a turntable called a 'scarf ring'.

In six months we were put through a rigorous course of cross-country flying over Scotland's beautiful, mountainous scenery. Aerobatics, air to ground strafing attacks, gunnery and bombing practice, navigation, air-to-air firing with two Vickers machine guns (firing straight forward through the propeller) and a free-firing Lewis gun in the rear compartment, meteorology and airmanship, both in the air and on the ground, and training in looking after the machines.

Kings Regulations (KR's) on RAF law were studied and there were lectures on the history of the RAF, although at that time this history was rather short, as the RAF having only begun on 1st April 1918, from the amalgamation of the RFC and the RNAS remaining from the First World War, only 20 years or so before.

About half way through our course the Air Ministry ordered night flying to become part of our training. Our instructors learnt first, with us huddled nervously in the back, and when they had become proficient, we swapped places. We took off and landed along a line of goose-neck flares, placed into wind. These consisted of watering cans with long spouts, filled with kerosene; a rag protruding out of the spout gave a reasonable flame. This was our flare-path. We had few instruments – airspeed, turn and bank indicator, altimeter and engine rev counter, but no artificial horizon or autopilot. Flying on cold, clear nights was thrilling in moonlight, when the ground was covered in snow. I especially enjoyed looping the loop over Dundee – a large town which was brightly lit up. One had only to stick the nose down to get up speed, pull the stick back with full throttle, cut off at the top and wait for the lights to appear again.

Once in daylight I tried to fly without oxygen at 23,000 feet, which made me feel happily drunk. I then passed out and came down in a screaming dive, just managing to pull out at 1,000 feet by using all my strength on the joystick. Never again without oxygen!

At the end of term, those of us who had attained the right grades attended a passing out parade and were presented with our wings – a proud moment. Having been given Xmas leave I drove my Fiat (1927 model) car to London, with one of my buddies, PO McFarlane, as co-driver. Unfortunately, in the early hours of the morning, in a murky mist, we collided with a lorry that had stopped by the roadside – a glancing blow, which shattered the windscreen and hood and caught the top of my head, scalping me as clean as any North American Indian would have done. Luckily I was wearing my leather flying helmet, but I was badly concussed. When the doctor took off the helmet there was a cascade of blood and the driver, my friend and fellow officer MacFarlane, promptly fainted and had to be seen to first.

I was taken to Peterborough Hospital and then to the RAF hospital at Uxbridge, Middlesex. P/O McFarlane, poor chap, was adjudged by the RAF to have been driving without due care and attention and, unbelievably, the cost of my training whilst I was in hospital was deducted monthly from his pay. This would have taken him years to pay off on our meagre pay, but became irrelevant when, as mentioned earlier, the unfortunate fellow was killed in a flying accident.

RAF Princess Royal nurses looked after me very well at Uxbridge and I made a good recovery. In the ward was a fellow pilot whose torso was covered in plaster except for a square opening in front, to allow a certain amount of expansion for food and drink. Several of us who were getting better used to slip out at quiet times, usually early evening, and hive off to the local pub – we knew when it was time to get back because the chap encased in plaster could only expand a certain amount though this aperture before he was liable to explode in agony!

Owing to my accident, I had to go back to No.8 FTS at Montrose to complete my training. At FTS I learnt the serious side of flying – it was a dangerous game if you took chances and didn't have your wits about you but the RAF training was second to none. Though sorry to leave Montrose, I was thrilled to be posted to 216 Squadron for a conversion course onto twin engined aircraft at Heliopolis, just outside Cairo in Egypt, in May 1937. Our course went out in a small troopship and you can imagine how thrilling it was for a bunch of young men to have the experience of calling in at various ports, Gibraltar, Marseilles, etc, on the way out. Few, if any of us, had been abroad before and here we were on a cruise of the Mediterranean at the expense of HM Government!

On arrival at Heliopolis we quickly settled in to the comfort of a first-class mess with large, airy rooms and an Egyptian attendant to look after us in the domestic quarters.

The Station Commander was Group Captain Raymond Cowleshaw, a WWI 'fighter ace'.

We trained on the Vickers 'Valencia' bomber/transport aircraft, a very slow open-cockpit biplane, known to us as 'Old Stringbag'. Its top speed was about 130 mph. It could carry 24 fully-armed soldiers when not used as a bomber. In spite of this, we enjoyed our six months, as the weather was perfect, though very hot at times. We got up at 4am and trained until 12 noon. After lunch and a siesta, sports activities continued until dinnertime. In the evenings we wore mess kit – blue trousers with white monkey jackets.

Peacetime flying out there was perfect. Visibility was excellent, except when sandstorms were about. The aircraft was robust and stable to fly, but took a long time to get anywhere, owing to its slow speed. At 10 to 15,000 feet the wind could exceed the speed of the aircraft, so it was quite a common occurrence to be flying backwards in relation to the ground! When visiting other aerodromes 'out in the sticks', re-fuelling was done by hand, with cans of petrol.

One of our tasks was to transport Army personnel from Khartoum to Port Said for their recreation by the sea. Stepping out of the aircraft at Khartoum was like stepping into a hot oven. I enjoyed these trips because we had to stay overnight in the Squadron Mess, which was a very pleasant experience. Before dinner, in the open air, a carpet was laid out in the garden with standard lamps at each corner. The officers gathered for cocktails in mess kit and the British Governor of Sudan would spend some time chatting with us. Then we would dine under a myriad of stars, with the mess silver gleaming in the light of silver table lamps with red silk shades.

On waking in my room, on one visit, there was a tarantula spider on the wall near my bed. I also visited Omdurman and the site of the battle of 1898, where I was quite surprised to see little boys and girls with ginger hair and pale skins, due, I was told, to the Scottish regiments in the Army at that time.

The local RAF Squadron was flying Wapiti aircraft and one of the favourite escapades after a mess party was to dive onto Sudanese Feluccas – local crescent-lateen-rigged sailing boats which were used on the Nile – and at the last moment execute a 'split-arse turn', thereby blowing the boat flat in the water. The boatmen would shake their fists, but little harm was done otherwise, but any pilot caught doing this in high spirits was in real trouble with his CO.

At the time, a large number of Abyssinian (Ethiopian) refugees were in evidence, due to their country having been invaded by the Italians, under their dictator Mussolini.

Life on the course with 216 Squadron was extremely pleasant. Our camp and aerodrome at Heliopolis was a few miles north of Cairo. We could walk out of the camp to the Heliopolis Sports Club, where we could use the outdoor pool in garden surroundings or walk a short distance further to enjoy dinner at the Heliopolis House Hotel, an elegant and splendid building. Outdoor cinemas were close by, where we could see all the latest Hollywood films under the stars at night and have snacks and drinks brought to us as we sat watching the films.

There was always plenty to do in Cairo, with its ancient monuments and the Citadel occupied by British Army HQ – as in those days Egypt was ruled by Britain as a protectorate (under the League of Nations, now the U.N.) in order to ensure the Suez Canal was safe for our ships to pass through to India. It was an important waterway for the British Empire.

Flying was a real pleasure, most of the time in clear sunny weather. On training flights down the Nile we were enthralled to see the pyramids as we flew down to Khartoum. The Squadron was responsible for policing the Suez Canal, which was interesting, and on occasions we had the chance of visiting Alexandria. While I was there I witnessed the 21st birthday of King Farouk, with all the magnificent celebrations. He was a handsome young man, very popular, and thought to have a brilliant future. Unfortunately, he became self-indulgent and made so many wrong moves that eventually he was deposed by his own people and died abroad in middle-age, through overindulgence and being grossly fat. Many years later, Budge and I were on holiday in Egypt and stayed in his Palace in Alexandria, which had been turned into a hotel, and were shown round his sleeping quarters. His uniforms and clothing were still in the wardrobes, so he must have left in a great hurry. News of his death came through while we were there and it went almost unnoticed in the Egyptian press – just a small paragraph. Nasser was President at the time.

Once I had a bit of luck. The Duff-Coopers (a Cabinet Minister VIP) were on an official visit from the UK and Lady Duff-Cooper had left her jewel case in Cairo when she was due to attend a ball in Alexandria. Her jewel case was brought to our aerodrome and I escorted the jewels on a night flight to Alex. It was a dark, moonless night but the sky was a mass of brilliant stars, like the diamonds I was carrying. We were in an open cockpit, affording an absolutely breathtaking view of myriads of stars above and the twinkling lights of the Nile Delta below.

[Although my father's description of life based in Heliopolis gives the impression of a trouble free tour of duty, the following extract from a letter to his wife, Budge, shows that some flights did not go according to plan! – P.M.A.A.]

216 B.T. Squadron, Helio. Cairo. Egypt

...My last letter ended in Khartoum I believe and now I am in a position to let you have the second instalment on this thrilling adventure in darkest Africa.

At 5.45 we took off and headed North on the morning of the 26th Thursday. After travelling for roughly 100 miles we developed engine trouble and decided to park down at a landing ground by station 10 on the Wadi Halfa – Khartoum Railway.

A safe landing was made in the burning desert. Time 11.30. We sent out a radio call and three hours later a plane popped down from Khartoum with a spare magneto (the trouble) and supplies of water and food.

However we could not leave that night so prepared to spend the night in the open.

The sun was scorching. The waves of heat that came up from the ground burned into my eyes and whole body, sapping nearly all my moisture. An hour before the relief plane arrived my throat was as dry as a bone.

Most of the men slept out on the sand while I collared a berth inside the aircraft. The seats can be raised and fixed into beds.

There was a range of blue rugged hills to the north which attracted my imagination. They appeared to change colour as the day advanced and I wondered if there were any strange tribesmen with fierce eyes protecting its secrets. They looked so mysterious.

Friday morning we were off before it became light, by breakfast we were at Wadfi Halfa where we procured lemonade and sandwiches. While driving to the hotel for grub I noticed the remains of that giant Italian airliner which crashed here and caught fire – some five weeks ago.

I was most annoyed at our forced landing because we had no time to stop at Luxor. A place I particularly wanted to see.

Helio was reached by two tired pilots, unwashed, at 6.30 Friday evening

Bomber Command Service

Having been converted onto twin-engine aircraft our course was returned to England and I was posted to 99 Squadron, based at Mildenhall near Newmarket in Suffolk. At that time I had an understanding with Budge, so on disembarkation leave I saw a lot of her. London was a wonderful place for young people and we went to the West End or locally to theatre and cinema shows or out to dinner dances at the Kit-Kat, Mayfair or Frascati's. We went dancing, sometimes for three or four nights in a row, without turning a hair, just taking it in our stride. Dinner Jackets were always worn, or full evening dress (tails), and the restaurants and hotels had glittering interiors and were luxuriously furnished. They were also not expensive; a whole evening would barely cost much more than a fiver.

At Mildenhall we shared the mess with 149 Squadron. Both squadrons were equipped with Handley Page Heyford Twin engined bombers of that period. They were (to us) huge biplanes, powered by two 600-hp Rolls Kestrel engines. They had an open cockpit and an open front compartment for an air gunner to operate a Lewis gun. Their top speed was little more than 120 mph, but they were proper bomb-carrying aircraft with a let down turret in the back fuselage, also equipped with a machine gun. There was no heating and at height in the winter they were extremely cold. We wore 'Sidcup' flying suits rather like those worn by Arctic explorers (from which they were copied) with fur collars and fur-lined boots, leather gloves with white double silk gloves inside and leather helmet and goggles. The aircraft had a fixed undercarriage with 'spats' half-covering the wheels. They looked as if they were flying upside down when in the air.

Shortly after going solo on one cross-country training session, a mist came down and obscured the countryside, so much so that I couldn't find our aerodrome. My petrol gauge showed I was running low so I picked a field and landed. I walked over to a farmhouse and phoned my unit. Our Flight Commander, Squadron Leader McKee (known as 'Square McKee' on the Squadron, who later became an Air Marshal and finally Governor of New Zealand after the war) came out and took over the controls. He taxied to the far end of the field, opened up the throttle and just cleared the hedge and trees at the other end.

Back at Mildenhall I only got a reprimand, as there was no damage to the aircraft. Personally, I thought I had done a great job by single-handedly landing this huge machine in a small field safely! As it was near a village called 'Little Port' I was ragged for days by my fellow officers in the mess with remarks like "any Little Port in a storm eh!"

Life was exciting and pleasant. We lived like lords as far as food was concerned, as Suffolk was full of game and fresh oysters were available on the coast nearby.

Our CO, Wing Commander H.E. Walker, was a short, stocky man who had been an RAF boxing champion in his younger days. Mildenhall contained 3 Group HQ and the AOC was a well-known WWI ace, AVM A.A. Thompson (know as 'Ack-Ack Thompson'). He was killed later, in tragic circumstances; while inspecting a new Hampden bomber on the tarmac he accidentally backed into a moving propeller when the bomb doors were opened unexpectedly.

Flying was a joy, except in cloud, as we had no artificial horizon. During a cross-country exercise in a thunderstorm, I experienced seeing "St Elmos Fire" – a weird, bluish light that glowed along the moving propeller, leading edges of the wings and other parts of the aircraft when our aircraft was struck by lightning.

We had numerous invitations from the local Landed Gentry near Mildenhall, who would arrange tennis parties at their Georgian mansions, for us to meet their daughters of marriageable age and to have tea on the lawns under cedar trees with servants and maids handing out muffins and ginger cream rolls and tea from silver urns. Most of us had our own girlfriends, so took little notice of those available, but greatly enjoyed the sport, tea and cakes.

We really had a great time, living the life of Riley!

In January 1938 the Squadron flew up to Evanton on attachment for air gunnery and bombing practice. This airfield is situated on the south side of the Moray Forth, just north of

Inverness, at the top end of Loch Ness, in the Scottish Highlands. We were there for 14 days, but this was cut short due to a terrific storm that blew up on the first Saturday, when I was orderly officer. The previous few days had been rough weather, with plenty of sleet and rain, but right from the start of Saturday morning it started to blow a gale, which increased until it became a wind of hurricane force – 70 to 80 mph. Our large Heyford bombers were in three lines at one end of the airfield, held down by iron 'screw pickets' under the lower wings. These were like giant corkscrews and were screwed firmly into the turf about 18 inches or so. The ground was very soft due to the rain and before long the planes began lifting off the ground as the gusts reached their flying speed of 60mph and loosened the pickets. We had placed lorries in front, to break the wind and stop the planes from pulling out of the ground as the wind increased, and I also called out every able-bodied person on the station to hang onto the leading edges of the Heyford wings to keep them down.

We had a floodlight brought up, which flooded the scene with a bright light and it was really weird to see these monster planes – which were, in fact, airborne – bouncing up and down, trying to get free. Eventually, one after the other, they pulled out the screw pickets and lifted off the ground, with loads of airmen dropping off the wings. The propellers were whirling round. The din was unimaginable, with the wind howling and bits of debris banging about, until finally, one after the other, these huge aircraft broke away and ended up in a heap at the boundary. Six of them were write-offs due to Mother Nature's tantrum.

Fortunately, 99 Squadron became the first squadron to be re-equipped with Wellingtons shortly afterwards and had the honour of carrying out operational trials with this new bomber to get over any "teething troubles". The famous Wellington bomber, affectionately known as the "Wimpey", was made by Vickers and designed by Barnes Wallace. Its airframe was of geodetic construction and could take a lot punishment and still get back to base. They were monoplanes and their speed was double that of the Heyfords. I loved their flying characteristics, for they were stable in flight and roomy to work in. the enclosed cockpit was a real blessing and, for the first time, we had an artificial horizon, which made flying in cloud no problem at all. An automatic pilot (George) was also a great boon on long flights.

In April 1939 I was sent on a 2nd class navigation course at Manston in Kent, which included Astro Navigation, and passed with high marks. On returning to 99 Squadron I obtained some leave and set off to France with P/O Kirby-Green in a borrowed long-nose SS Jaguar. There were four of us in two cars and we arranged to meet at Biarritz, close to the Spanish border. Kirby-Green and I took it in turns to drive and expected we would meet the other car frequently on the way down, but not a bit of it – we didn't see them until we arrived at Biarritz. My recollection, although a bit hazy now, was of seeing a beautiful town with elegant, spacious hotels, a beautiful beach and colourful gardens, built on the Atlantic Coast in the 19th Century.

We decided to take a look at Spain and set off southwards, reaching the frontier after lunching at a small restaurant in St. Jean-de-Luz, where we feasted on the most delicious grilled sardines, a speciality of that region. However, our plans were dashed to the ground by the Spanish Frontier Police, who said "Non, non," whilst wagging a finger and looking at our passports. "Ingles Pilots... Civil war in Spain, Señors."

Though disappointed we made for St. Raphael on the French Riveira. Half way there, not far from Toulouse, as I was dozing in the passenger seat, we swerved and went over a small wall, landing below in a semi dried-up river. Kirby-Green said a dog had run in front of the car. The whole of the roof was ripped off and though concussed by the bang from the drop, we sat there laughing our heads off. Kirby-Green was just badly shaken, but I needed attention for concussion and was taken to a convent hospital with a badly lacerated hand and face.

The nurses were nuns in full rig-out and most attentive to our needs. One diminutive nun with a sweet young face took my temperature – in the continental way, which took me by surprise, with an instrument which looked rather like a poker with a wooden handle. She wielded this so skilfully that before I knew what was happening it was 'whoops, what the hell do you think you're playing at?'

Holidays are not meant for staying in hospitals so on the third day K-G and I legged it to the station when all was quiet in siesta time and met our friends in St. Raphael, where we stayed at a very nice hotel on the front. We chummed up with a couple of South African Army officers and all six spent our time on the beach. My complete arm and hand was bandaged and I had to hold it up above the water when swimming. Of course, all the people lying on the beach, young and old, thought I was waving to them, so as I went along, they all waved back!

Everything was fun and carefree. One of our company got severe sunstroke, so we sat him up in bed with an ice-pack on his head and sent for the hotel's French doctor. Meantime another of our group had far too much Pernod before lunch so we had to take him back to the hotel. At the precise moment that he was finding it difficult to get through the entrance doorway, the Doctor arrived and carted him off, thinking he was the casualty with sunstroke, leaving the suffering patient sitting in bed with the ice pack on his head.

On the train back to Calais we wined and dined exceedingly well in the restaurant car, too well in fact, and ran out of money for the ferry. We got on board quite easily without tickets, but throughout the voyage we were only a step or two ahead of the ticket inspector. Then I had an incredible stroke of luck. I spotted a chap who was in another Squadron based at Mildenhall who had a real floozy on his arm and I rightly surmised that he had spent a "dirty weekend" in Paris. In those days peccadilloes of this kind were kept secret, especially where parents were concerned. If found out, all hell was usually let loose. The upshot of it all was that he couldn't give me the money fast enough for the fare on the ferry and train to London, on condition that I wouldn't split on him. Call it blackmail if you like, but I figured that it was all in a good cause.

On my arrival home, Budge told me that a friend of hers had told her she was so sorry to hear that I had died in a car accident in France. It had been reported as such in one of the daily papers. Some reporter in that region had jumped to the wrong conclusion, probably because the car was a complete write-off and the bodies were never found in the river.

Around this time the RAF staged a demonstration to convey the message to Germany that we had long-range aircraft capable of reaching Berlin and returning. Along with other squadrons, we flew in squadron formation from Mildenhall to Paris, where we flew three-abreast down the Champs Elysees and over the Arc de Triumph at 200 feet; from there to Marseilles and back – non-stop and with fuel to spare. It was a thrilling experience for me to be on such a long flight, of some 8 hours, especially to see Paris and Marseilles at such close quarters in daylight. It was well publicised by the continental media, but made little difference to Hitler's plans for expansion in Europe.

Aircraft in use in the early days of RAF Bomber Command

Fairey Battle

Armstrong Whitworth Whitley
powered by twin Armstrong Siddeley Tiger 1x Radials Mk.I

Bristol Blenheim ~ Type 142.

3. The War ~ 1939-45

This heavenly, enjoyable life came to an end during that long, hot summer of 1939, as we perfected our training on Wellingtons. The aerodrome and hangers were camouflaged and we were put 'on war footing'. All leave was cancelled and slit trenches were dug. Strange women in air force blue uniforms arrived without prior notice. We had never seen them before and didn't have a clue as to their purpose (other than what comes naturally!) This was the first contingent of the WAAF. Training intensified and we were not allowed to go more than 2½ hours away from camp. The Munich crisis in 1938 gave us just enough breathing space to improve our armed forces to some extent, but Germany had already armed fully and had annexed Austria and later marched into Czechoslovakia.

Two days before war was declared, 99 Squadron was moved to Newmarket Racecourse and operated from the Rowley Mile gallop, a large, grassed area beside the racecourse. The jockey's weighing-in room was our operations and communications room and most personnel slept in the grandstand. The Royal WC was placed at our disposal!

On 3rd September 1939, I, along with fellow aircrew, was sitting on the steps of the grandstand, listening to Neville Chamberlain, the Prime Minister, announce on the radio that because Hitler had refused to withdraw his troops from Poland, Britain was now at war with Germany. Although we knew that precautions in case of war breaking out had been taken nationally, the speed of events took us by surprise. Few people knew we even *had* a treaty with

Poland until it was announced on the radio, so it came as a tremendous shock to us that we were now 'on the front line', as it were.

Based on First World War information and stories, the average aircrew expected to last only a few weeks in combat. But, to our surprise, nothing very much happened to begin with. A black-out was imposed and the Army moved into our part of East Anglia, turning the whole area into an armed camp. Operational aircraft were now 'dispersed' around airfield perimeters in concrete bays, instead of being kept in hangars, but other than this, training continued as usual.

On 29th September I and Budge were married by special licence; very costly – 25 shillings (£1.25p). I managed to get three days leave and motored down to Seaford, near Brighton on the South Coast, in my Triumph (aluminium bodied) sports car, which had a real throaty roar. Budge's mother had a holiday bungalow there. We were married in a lovely old stone-built church by an elderly vicar. During the service I noticed a rather strong smell of alcohol, which I assumed to be emanating from the vicar. When we left for the reception in a nearby hotel I mentioned this to my bride, who burst out laughing and I noticed that the pungent aroma was still with us. She explained that her mother had given her a shot of brandy to sustain her during the service – and there I was accusing the poor old vicar!

I was in uniform with the one thick stripe of a Flying Officer on my sleeve and I had to be back at Newmarket for flying duties the following day. We had a splendid lunch at the Cumberland Hotel in Eastbourne but on the way to Stevenage I managed to drive into the back of a bus, albeit not very seriously. The conductor shook his head slowly but let us off after observing all the ribbons and tin cans attached to the car and Budge looking radiant by my side. Our honeymoon was spent at the Crown Hotel in Stevenage and the girl receptionist, on seeing lovely Budge all dressed up and sparkling with jewellery, took me aside and explained *sotto voce* that this was the night of a country-wide census, when everyone had to fill in a form as to whom they were with. She probably had previous experience of RAF servicemen week-ending with their girlfriends and wanting to keep their liaisons quiet (as was the form in those days) and was trying to warn me of the situation, but I was rather put out and informed her, somewhat haughtily, that we had been properly married that day and that I was surprised that she should think otherwise. She probably didn't believe me anyway!

We had a superb evening meal and then retired for our honeymoon night to a large bedroom with an en-suite bathroom. I undressed in the bathroom and when Budge was in bed I emerged in pyjamas and got into bed in the dark. (From what others have told me, such first-night shyness was quite the norm in those days.) As it turned out, the night proved hilarious. We woke in the small hours, sweltering in a temperature of something like 85 degrees. The newly-installed central heating boiler had apparently gone wrong and the whole system was bubbling and gurgling out of control. I had hoped our honeymoon would be pretty hot stuff but I didn't think it would be as hot as that!

Then it was back to Newmarket, 99 Squadron and the war.

The Wellington was the heavy bomber of that period and we were well trained in formation flying. For hours and hours we practised close formation flying, almost wingtip to wingtip, like fighters, the idea being that we could defend ourselves from fighters by cross-fire from the whole formation. We aircrew felt well trained and believed we had the finest aircraft in the world. We couldn't imagine suffering the level of losses experienced over the Western front in WWI. Personally, I never doubted I would survive aerial combat; I was so confident in our aircraft and training that I never wrote a letter to my wife in case I didn't survive. Quite a lot of aircrew did this, as I learnt later in the war, when I had to deal with them myself.

We were, of course, overconfident; we had no idea what the German Air Force and anti-aircraft defences were like or what they could do to us.

During the 'Phoney War' (September 1939 to May 1940) nothing catastrophic happened. The British Expeditionary Force was established alongside the French and Belgian armies. French troops manned the Maginot Line of fortifications facing Germany and the Germans manned the Siegfried Line of fortifications facing the French.

Now and then our radar had picked up a high-flying German reconnaissance aircraft approaching from the East across the North Sea and so as to fool them, our squadrons based in Norfolk and Suffolk were instructed to fly inland to more westerly airfields, presumably so that they couldn't estimate our strength. We carried our camp beds and overnight kit in our aircraft and usually slept in airport buildings, such as they were at that time. Night flying became more difficult because of the nationwide blackout and radio fixes were unreliable in bad weather.

On 9th October 1939 I was posted to St Athan, near Barry in South Wales, to the specialist Navigation Course. Off we went merrily in my Triumph sports car and settled into digs in a private house, only to be driven out a short time after by the landlady, who objected to us opening any windows for ventilation. A kind local policeman got us rooms in a large house on the shore of the Bristol Channel at Breaksea point. It was in an elegant Georgian house with bungalows in the grounds let to Air Force Officers. We had a lovely drawing room with a large old fire grate of that period, which consumed coal at great speed. In order to economise, Budge, my young, inexperienced bride, reduced the capacity of the grate by lining it with large, rounded stones she had found on the beach outside – and nearly blew the house up. Shortly after having lit the fire it exploded as if a bomb had gone off in it. Fragments of stone were all over the place. It then dawned on us that these large stones were made of flint, which had exploded in the heat of the fire with devastating effect.

The course took three months and went into advanced navigation, including Astro, which was only just coming into use. We flew day and night in Anson twin-engined aircraft, perfecting the navigation skills of the period. I think Budge knew as much as I did on my passing out as a 1st class Navigator, because she and I practised the ghastly spherical trigonometry formulae together and she had a better memory than me.

During the course I had another accident with my car, involving a service vehicle from the camp. I wasn't insured, as I had lost my driving licence some months previously through arguing with a local magistrate who had the temerity to increase my fine every time I opened my mouth to persuade him otherwise. Fortunately, a friendly warrant officer in the transport section of the station took pity on me and allowed the embarrassing incident to go unrecorded, otherwise I might have faced a court martial.

I returned to Newmarket and 99 Squadron on 5th February 1940 and found the situation had changed drastically. The previous December, 99 Squadron had been sent out in daylight to attack units of the German Fleet near Heligoland, off the north German coast, at the request of the Admiralty. As previously described, we had been trained to fly in close formation, almost wing-tip to wing-tip for mutual protection, relying on the combined fire power of our gunners to beat off enemy fighter attacks. The first raid went off fairly well and although one or two were lost, either through a concentration of fire from 'Flak' ships, or attack by fighters, the bomber formation held together reasonably well, even shooting down one or two of the attacking fighters.

The second raid to the same area was totally different. Twelve of 99 Squadron's aircraft were sent out, again to attack units of the German fleet in daylight. This time the number of Flak ships had been increased and the FREYA radar system picked up the bombers some 70 miles off the coast. As a result the formation was met by a horde of the latest fighters armed with cannons (which were not fitted to the earlier lot) and more concentrated fire from the Flak ships. Six were shot down in flames and one badly damaged plane crashed just short of base at Newmarket.

I lost some good friends that day, with whom I had trained for 2½ years. Other squadrons in No.3 Group shared a similar fate. To have seven out of twelve in the formation destroyed was a terrible blow to the squadron and No.3 Group as a whole. This harsh lesson was not lost on the Air Ministry and it was decided that the losses likely to be incurred through daylight attacks could not be sustained and Bomber Command rightly turned to night operations for penetration into enemy territory.

My posting to the Navigation specialist course at St Athan in Wales undoubtedly saved me, as I would otherwise have been on those disastrous raids.

Budge and I lived in a pretty little cottage on the main road leading north out of Newmarket in the direction of Bury St Edmunds. The owners, Mr and Mrs Hammond, lived in the big house up a drive from the cottage. They were a lovely couple; he owned the Humber car agency and riding stables in Newmarket High Street.

Newmarket was attacked several times by sneak raiders when there was a low cloud base. On one of these raids a Dornier 217 bomber dropped a stick of HE bombs right down the High Street. One bomb demolished a building containing a flat that Budge and I had viewed a short time before, but which I had rejected because I had a premonition, in the form of a feeling of dread and an icy atmosphere when we were viewing. I heard this raider's machine guns firing as he came down the main road and I blazed away at him with my revolver. Quite ineffectual, no doubt, but it made me feel good. This raid killed and wounded a lot of people.

Newmarket was also attacked at night with "screaming" bombs, which the Luftwaffe used as terror weapons. They were normal bombs with "whistle" devices attached, which made a terrifying screaming noise as they dropped. Budge had many friends among my fellow officers' wives, as they all used to play squash regularly together. They were all in their early twenties and found it heart-rending trying to comfort the wives whose husbands had been reported missing. They were a close-knit and happy band of young women but gradually lost touch as the war progressed and their husbands were posted away. Life altered quickly in wartime and situations changed rapidly.

On 13th February 1940 I was posted to RAF Stradishall to join 214 Squadron. This had been a WW1 Squadron in the RNAS and became 214 Squadron on 1st April 1918, when the Royal Air Force was formed. RAF Stradishall was the first 3 Group Bomber Station to have concrete runways, which made take-offs and landings much smoother for heavily loaded aircraft. When I arrived it was an operational training station and, having just finished a Spec Nav course, I was appointed Squadron Navigation Officer in addition to the duties of an operational pilot. This did not last long before the squadron gained full operational status and bombing missions began.

The situation at that time was that in April, May and June, Germany attacked and overran Norway, Holland and lastly through Belgium into France, which surrendered. The British Expeditionary Force was driven out of France at Dunkirk. What was left of the RAF squadrons in France flew back and ground-crews struggled back alongside the Army soldiers – if they were lucky enough to be rescued off the beaches by the Navy. The British Army lost most of its tanks, artillery and transport and was virtually ineffective. The Navy had its hands full dealing with the German U-boat problem and protecting the convoys across the Atlantic, which was Britain's lifeline for supplies of food and equipment. Now Britain stood alone, facing the might of Hitler's Germany. The only armed force left to carry the fight to the enemy was RAF Bomber Command.

Both Fighter Command and Bomber Command were small in numbers to start with. From May to the end of September Fighter Command defeated the Luftwaffe in the Battle of Britain, repelling the attacks that were intended as a precursor to the invasion of Britain. In the meantime, Bomber Command wasted no time in starting to weaken German aggression by making attacks on her means of production of armaments, communications and naval forces.

My first tour on operations lasted through 1940 until March 1941. Most of our targets were in the Ruhr, the industrial heartland of Germany, and others within a radius of 600 miles, which included the Berlin and Magdeburg areas. The channel ports were also attacked when masses of transport barges were assembled ready for the invasion.

The typical routine was for the aircrew to report to their flights at 10.00 hrs each day to find out which crews would be on 'ops' that night, the rest being "stood down". As Captain along with my co-pilot I would have a word with the groundcrew who serviced and bombed-up our aircraft, check everything, fly a couple of circuits on test, then go into the mess for lunch. Briefing would be at 1400 hrs and the CO would reveal the target and details of take-off times. Then the specialists would run through their information and instructions. The Intelligence officer would give details of 'Flak' (anti-aircraft) bands across Germany and estimated strength of flak over the target, followed by the signals officer dealing with airfield identification beacons, colours of the day, German radio frequencies, radar locations, enemy night-fighter areas, etc. The Met Officer would give the expected weather en route and over the target, also landing conditions on return and wind-speed and direction at various heights en route and over the target.

After "any questions" the briefing ended and each navigator worked out the route to the target on his charts. The Captain then went through the whole trip with the crew, reminding them about rations, effect of cold and fatigue and the need to carry oxygen bottles at height when moving about the aircraft and other safety precautions in case we were shot down or had to land in the sea. We all carried silk maps sewn into the linings of our clothes and compasses disguised as buttons or shirt collar studs to help us to escape, which we were expected to do if captured.

Our point of departure was Southwold on the Suffolk coast and all routes out and back started at that place on the chart, so that hopefully the enemy would not know from which airfield the aircraft had started. A time was set to assemble in the crew room when the crew members were expected to be ready for a truck to take them to the aircraft. If time allowed we would go to our rooms and sleep or rest and have a pre-flight meal before taking off individually at the appointed time.

From then on we were on our own, each aircraft proceeded to the target independently in my day, carried out its mission and returned, hopefully unscathed, anywhere between three or eight hours later, depending on the target distance. Crews became close-knit, each relying on each other's skills for the safety of the whole crew. In the air, the designated captain of the aircraft was the boss and gave the orders, irrespective of rank.

On our return there would be a de-briefing session with the Intelligence staff, then a very welcome breakfast of bacon and eggs, followed by bed and oblivion. Sorties were usually every third night but a lot were cancelled due to bad weather, especially during winter months, which often produced $10/10^{ths}$ cloud over Europe. Under these conditions we had to bring our bomb-load back if the target could not be identified. On one particular sortie in atrocious weather I flew for some six hours in cloud and brought back my bomb-load as instructed as the target could not be identified. Being shot at in cloud over flak lines gave one a feeling of utter helplessness.

Weather forecasts were not always very good and I personally was worried more by the prospect of bad weather conditions than enemy actions. Returning to base early one morning after a raid on a difficult target in the Ruhr, I was faced with locating Stradishall in a violent thunderstorm and only got down by spotting the runway through a small gap in the clouds, when it was illuminated by multiple flashes of lightning.

On another occasion several aircraft in our group were lost due to their altimeters giving their pilots a false height above ground. The barometric pressure had altered significantly during their flight and when they returned in the dark with the cloud-base very low, they believed themselves to be at a very much higher altitude than they actually were. The Colston altimeter was accurate down to 10 feet, but only if the current barometric pressure of the aerodrome was known and set manually. This problem was overcome by returning aircraft obtaining the correct pressure to adjust the altimeter by radio before approaching a base at night or letting down through low cloud day or night. If there was a wide variation of pressure, the altimeter could give the pilot a false reading as much as 1,000 feet in extreme cases.

Flying for many hours on instruments in cloud greatly tested a pilot's endurance to the limit. In cumulonimbus – heavy thunder clouds – the buffeting and turbulence was great enough to throw the Wellington all over the place and in extreme conditions it could topple the gyro of the artificial horizon. If this happened one was pretty well a "gonner" unless one was lucky enough to come out of cloud and actually have enough light to see the ground say, by moonlight and also have enough height to pull out of the dive before hitting the ground.

During the war, of course, both England and Germany were totally blacked out at night, so nothing could be identified apart from coastlines, rivers and lakes and then with great difficulty, except in moonlight. Targets were heavily defended by anti-aircraft batteries coordinated with searchlights; clear weather was good for identification and bombing of targets but also good for the flak batteries and searchlights. If an aircraft was caught by one searchlight all the others in the area would "lock-on". If the flak batteries then stopped firing it was certain that night fighters were closing in for the kill.

My Wellington was caught once and it was a nasty experience. I was doing the bomb aiming in the front turret during which my second Pilot had to fly straight and level for several minutes on the run-up to the target. I had just released the bomb-load when we were caught in an intense white light. It was weird; everything inside the plane was lit up but we couldn't see anything outside. I crawled back to the cockpit and saw P/O Hartford, my second pilot, staring straight ahead, transfixed in an absolute daze. I yelled at him and broke the spell, then yanked him out of his seat, took his place and threw the aircraft all over the sky until I was out of the light and away.

On most of my sorties we sustained minor damage but nothing vital. The nearest I got to being wounded was when a piece of red-hot shrapnel embedded itself in my parachute, which I was sitting on. Once I hit a balloon cable when returning from a mission. Fortunately, we had cable-cutting cartridges on the leading edges of our wings, which exploded and blew the cable apart. Nevertheless, the aircraft stalled and fell a few thousand feet before I was able to pull it out of a screaming dive, luckily in bright moonlight. On another sortie to the Stettin area, after dealing with the target I turned north to fly over the Baltic and was amazed to see Sweden all lit up – a boon in helping us pinpoint our position.

In the first part of my operational tour Budge and I lived in a farmhouse and it was my practice on returning from a mission to fly low over the dwelling to let Budge know I was back safely. She would open the bedroom window, as it was usually very early in the morning, and lean out and wave her handkerchief and I would waggle my wings in salute. My crew were young and barely out of their teens and on one occasion I looked round to see them gawping excitedly out of the aircraft windows at my very scantily dressed bride in her diaphanous nightie. I had wondered why, on previous such occasions, I had had to adjust the trim of the aircraft; it was on account of them all being on one side! Over the intercom I shouted "Eyes front!" but couldn't help chuckling as I did so.

Later on in the year we moved to an Elizabethan farmhouse which we swore was haunted. There was a loft at the top of the house where apples were stored. The door had a spring catch, the latch of which had to be forced down with considerable effort against the spring for it to open. We were given permission to take the apples and we were particular to shut the door on coming away. But no matter how many times we locked the spring catch on the door, we always found it open. This 16th century old house had an oak-studded door leading from a wide hall into the garden at the back. Later on, in 1940, the German Army was being assembled to invade Britain and we were alerted to the possibility of German parachute troops landing in Suffolk prior to invasion. Suddenly, one night, we heard heavy knocking sounds on this door and saw it shake with blows on the outside. It stopped as suddenly as it started, then the vibrations were repeated several times, then stopped. We were scared stiff, to put it mildly, and the hairs at the back of my neck (hackles) literally stood up. Unable to stand the suspense any longer I rushed out, brandishing my revolver, only to find not a soul about – a remarkable phenomenon for which I had no explanation. On returning to the house I was almost equally frightened to be met by Budge, brandishing a poker and ready to do battle with the enemy!

In November 1940 I was awarded my first Distinguished Flying Cross (DFC), which was recommended by my CO, Wing Commander J.E. Nuttall and the station Commander Group Captain S.B. Harris and finally by the Group Commander of No.3 Group at Mildenhall, Air Vice Marshal J.E. (Jackie) Baldwin. The citation is given in Appendix A. King George VI presented this award at a ceremony held in a hanger at Stradishall and whilst pinning it on my tunic, with difficulty, he said, "I s-say, t-this is a n-n-no g-good p-pin, i-isn't it?" (poor chap stuttered rather badly). Afterwards he, with Queen Elizabeth (later the Queen Mother) and their two daughters, Princesses Elizabeth and Margaret, had lunch with us in the Mess. A memorable day.

It was about this time that London was heavily bombed by the Luftwaffe and as a result the RAF had permission to include Berlin as a target, with its factories, government buildings (Nazi HQ), railway marshalling yards, power plants, etc. I was on one of the first raids and my target was a large gas producing plant. It was a successful trip in good weather and later, by request of the BBC, I made a broadcast from London of that experience. This raid was described in a wartime book, *Wings of Victory*, a tribute to the RAF by Ivor Halstead, of which I still have a copy.

The reality of being pitched into serious warfare against a ruthless enemy in the skies over Europe became a hard slog. At the end of my tour (normally 30 missions or 300 operational hours) I had lost most of my friends, either killed or "in the bag" (shot down and taken prisoner). At the start of the war we aircrews (all volunteers) had been well trained and had great faith in ourselves and our aircraft, but after a few missions anxiety would gradually build up as each new sortie approached, developing slowly throughout the day before take-off into the dark night to seek targets that we knew would be difficult to identify and heavily defended.

Surviving this war in the air was a matter of luck. Like me, one could go through two tours of highly dangerous operations over enemy territory and not get a scratch, but if your aircraft was badly damaged by flak or fighters or you ran into foul weather, then you were in dead trouble. The odds were loaded against your survival. Nevertheless, we all knew precisely what we were fighting for, were supremely confident in our skills and had great loyalty to our squadrons and the Royal Air Force.

At the end of February 1941 I was promoted to Squadron Leader and posted to HQ Bomber Command when Air Marshal Sir Richard Pierce was C-in-C. I served in the Navigation Section, which had the duties of advising the C-in-C on matters concerning the best routes for navigators to take to their targets in relation to the bands of anti-aircraft and searchlights that extended over the whole of Germany and to advise on the moon phases and any new navigational aids being developed. The whole of Bomber Command's strategy emanated from the C-in-C in this vast building, hidden underground in the woods in Buckinghamshire. I thoroughly enjoyed this experience.

In case of invasion or attack by enemy paratroops we, the headquarters staff, were incorporated into a company called the Southdown Rifles and were issued with rifles. A real laugh and thank God we were never put to the test! Air Marshal (Bomber)

Harris took over as C-in-C while I was there. Sometimes I dealt with him personally and found him direct and firm with a "no nonsense" atmosphere about him. No wonder he commanded respect. Bomber Command aircrew held him in great regard.

Budge was quite put out when I was first posted to Bomber Command, as she was heavily pregnant, but brightened up when she learnt I had been promoted to Squadron Leader. When Penelope was born on 11th March 1941 I managed to borrow a De Havilland Rapide twin-engined passenger plane from the communications flight at Halton and flew up to Newmarket to see her. The Nursing Home was closed when I got there but I managed to get in through Budge's window, much to her surprise and delight. Matron made a great fuss of us both and I was able to see Penelope, our newly born babe, which was wonderful, before returning the next day.

Allied Strategic Air Command – Overseas

At the end of March 1942 I was posted to a newly-formed Squadron – No.159 at Polebrook near Peterborough – where we converted onto American B24s – four-engined bomber aircraft known in the RAF as 'Liberators'. These were much larger and faster than Wellingtons, with double the range. They were much more roomy to walk about in and the pilot's seat was like a comfortable armchair. They had self-sealing petrol tanks in the wings and were well armed with gun turrets in the tail, mid-upper (fuselage), nose and a machine gun on either side of the rear fuselage. Just before going to Lineham, 159 Squadron was attached to 120 Squadron Coastal Command, where, for a short period, we operated to test out the endurance of our 'Libs' on long sorties. We flew to Northern Ireland to RAF Nutts Corner, an aerodrome right by Lough Neagh, near Belfast. Our job was to fly out to mid-Atlantic, pick up an incoming convoy and look out for and deal with German U-boat submarines intent on attacking and sinking the ships. On one of these missions one of our squadron located a convoy in low cloud condition and fired off recognition signals of the day but the "trigger happy" Navy blasted off with all their anti aircraft weapons and unfortunately the rear gunner was killed by a direct hit, which left only part of his turret intact. Who can blame them given their terrible losses? Besides, they had not seen an Allied 4-engined aircraft before. The Lib was probably mistaken for a German Condor – a four engined bomber which operated alongside the U-Boat packs.

After our brief attachment to Coastal Command's 120 Squadron we were ordered to RAF Station Lineham, near Swindon in Wiltshire, the base from which the RAF dispatched squadrons going overseas. During my short stay there I had terrible nightmares and was told by my 'batwoman' that a pilot had committed suicide in my room a few weeks before. WAAFs had now taken over the traditionally male job of the batman and it was a new experience to have a female look after us.

I was 'B' Flight Commander in 159 Squadron; Wing Commander Skinner was our CO and Squadron Leader Max Boffee the 'A' Flight Commander. The Squadron had orders to proceed overseas to India via Gibraltar and Egypt. The CO was delighted to have the opportunity of going back there, as he had spent many years in India in the RAF and was particularly fond of 'pig-sticking hunts' with lances on horseback, hunting wild boar – a popular sport in certain parts of North India. Sadly, he never got to enjoy this sport again, as he was shot down over Rangoon in Burma later in 1943.

Our time at Lineham was spent preparing for the long flights ahead and for going on active operations when we arrived at our destination, this time against the Japs, who had recently declared war on Britain and the USA with the surprise Pearl Harbor attack and had joined the Axis Powers with Germany. Much care was taken testing the turrets and sighting the guns, checking the operation of the bomb-doors (which rolled up either side of the bomb bay in the fuselage, rather like a roller desk), checking bomb racks, flare chutes, all equipment stowed in the aircraft, radio and navigation equipment, compasses and a hundred and one other checks, besides loading many belts of .303 ammunition for our Browning machine guns.

An amusing incident occurred when my CO asked me to accompany him to look round our aircraft. He was very particular to check everything. As we came round the port wing he noticed a thin stream of liquid coming off the trailing edge of the wing. He put his hand out and tested it by smell.

"Just as I thought," he said. "The tail is down a bit and this is petrol overflowing from full tanks."

We then proceeded to walk towards the rear compartment when he saw a thin stream of similar liquid coming from the underneath onto the ground. He went over and collected some onto his hand, sniffed it, tasted it, turned to me and said, "I can't make this out, its not a lubricant and furthermore it's slightly warm. Get in and find out where it's coming from and what it is – it might be important."

I did as he requested and just as I entered the rear compartment I heard one of our maintenance crew say, "Stop pissing Bert – the CO's outside!" Need I say more!

Budge came over to see me off. She was staying with her mother at Bedford Park, Chiswick and had driven down in our little car with Penelope all on her own. There were no signposts on the roads in wartime and she had successfully map-read her way to Lineham – no easy task for a young bride with a baby. She really showed some pluck in doing this.

Towards the end of April or early May 1942 the Squadron was ready and Wing Commander Skinner detailed me to go off first, entrusting me to test the short runway at Gibraltar before committing the whole Squadron. First I had to fly out to Hurn (Bournemouth Airport) to weigh the aircraft and find out its centre of gravity. I had assumed that the aircraft was properly fuelled up for the short flight (famous last words) and didn't check and I was very lucky to get there. I was crosswind, ready to turn in to land at about 1,000 feet when my engines started to splutter and one after the other they cut out, just as I landed. I kept quiet about it, but never forgot the lesson.

At Hurn we refuelled and took off with a full load, including two crews – our 159 Squadron ones and a second crew for 160 Squadron who we were ferrying out to wait until they got their own aircraft. We were kitted out with tropical gear and carried our camp beds with us, so our aircraft was crammed with personnel and their gear.

I flew out to some 14 degrees west in the Atlantic then turned south to close in on Portugal at Cape St Vincent, before turning south-east on the last leg to Gibraltar.

Without brakes, a Liberator could run for three miles and at the briefing beforehand there was some humour, at my expense, when they said the strip at Gibraltar was easy to recognise as you could see all the high tails of Wellingtons which had overshot the runway sticking out of the water on either side of the narrow isthmus joining the Rock to the mainland.

I approached over the bay of Algeciras with full flap, just above stalling speed, and cut the throttles right back just before the wheels touched the runway. With brakes full on I managed to stop some 10 yards from the sea at the other end, much to the relief of the crew. Half of Gibraltar had turned out to witness the first landing of a four-engine bomber. Amongst the crowd was an old schoolfriend, Captain Hay, who was a gunner stationed on the Rock. I took him up on one of my test runs and scared the daylights out of him, as both take-off and landing were hairy experiences. Afterwards he said that he was glad he was in the Army! In return he took me round the secret tunnels in the Rock and showed me the Barbary Apes which live there.

I stayed three nights at the famous Rock Hotel and one evening a naval officer took me down to have a look at the docks and warships in the bay. The Navy was having a very bad time during this period with their convoys supplying Malta. With little air cover they were getting a real pasting from the Luftwaffe and hardly any ships were getting through to Malta. The ratings were taking the brunt and were no longer saluting their officers, I noticed. However, they were not mutinous and the Naval Command turned a blind eye to this as they knew what a strain they were under.

Having signalled back to my CO that with great care it was safe to land Liberators at Gibraltar I took off again for Egypt, climbing to 15,000 feet. After 20 minutes or so I looked out of the port window and saw an aircraft carrier limping back to Gibraltar. I'm not sure whether it was the *Illustrious* or the *Eagle*, which were doing the Malta runs at that period. I took the route over Tunisia and down the centre of the Med to Cairo, where we landed at LG (landing ground) 224, to be greeted by masses of flies, which descended on us in a cloud. On arrival instead of going on to India, Churchill, our bulldog Prime Minister gave orders for us to be attached to 205 Group to operate from Fayid RAF aerodrome on the Bitter Lakes on the Suez Canal. There we were to operate as part of the allied strategic Air Force. This made sense, as the German Afrika Korps had taken over from the Italians in Libya and was on its way to Cairo.

Our task was to bomb entry ports into Libya to slow-down or destroy ships and supplies of fuel, food and armaments – to prevent them reaching Rommel's army – and to attack enemy troop concentrations and communications in the desert. This we did, along with other squadrons of Wellingtons, Blenheims and Mitchells, in conjunction with the newly-formed No.1 Tactical (Desert) Air Force, which operated solely with the Army, using fighters and light bombers. The whole of our Air Force effort was to gain superiority in the air for the protection of the 8th Army holding the Afrika Korps at bay.

For six months 159 Squadron operated in this theatre of war by night and by day. The weather was perfect except in sandstorms and night bombing was accurate as targets were mostly on the coast and quite easily identified. From Fayid we attacked targets as far away as Italy (Taranto Naval base) and Crete (which German paratroops had recently taken). Fixed targets such as ports were ringed with flak batteries, which sent up a hefty barrage of shells directly over our targets and we had no option but to fly through them on our bombing runs. Their trouble was to get our height accurately. This was our saving grace. Daylight attacks were much worse owing to running battles with fighters before and after.

Our Liberators could sustain quite a lot of damage without going down. My aircraft was hit on numerous sorties and after one sortie on Tobruk we were attacked by a night fighter, which my rear gunner dealt with efficiently enough to make him fade away in the darkness, but not before he had sprayed our aircraft with bullets. Again we were fortunate, as nothing vital was hit. The mid-upper gunner was lucky, as he got a bullet through the length of the sole of his shoe but otherwise got off scot-free.

Daylight missions were very different. We had no fighter air cover so we flew in formation to give mutual support in firepower. To get under the German radar screen we flew low down the Med or down the Quattara Depression (a vast stretch of land below sea-level, which runs westwards for hundreds of miles south of the coastal strip) then at the last minute we would climb as rapidly as possible to bombing height for the final attack. We could not escape detection as we neared the target and it was sickening to have to witness the fighters taking off from their desert airstrips as we approached. Meantime the rings of anti-aircraft defences were being manned to put up a terrific barrage over our target.

This happened on 23rd July 1942 on one of my sorties against shipping and port installations at Benghazi in Libya. We had flown for six hours 100 feet up over the bottom of the Quattara Depression and climbed up to 18,000 feet south of Benghazi. At that height I could see the fighters taking off to attack us. Then, way above us, on our run up to the docks, I saw a formation of American Liberators attack right in front. They had supercharged engines, so could fly at 32,000 feet, out of flak range (their Nordyn bombsight was better than ours in the RAF) and I was amazed to see a large cargo ship in the docks receive a direct hit. It just exploded upwards and outwards with complete destruction.

We were all tensed up in my formation, naturally, and on the approach it was like watching a film in slow motion. The noise of the engines blanked out most sounds except directions "left... left..." or "right... right..." from the bomb aimer or information from the gunners of fighter activity over the intercom system. Then all hell was let loose as we flew through the dense flak barrage. I could hear the crump, crump of shells exploding all around us and see the black puffs of smoke. The sound was somewhat like heavy doors being slammed at the end of an echoing corridor at each burst. Then "bombs away" and shortly afterwards my rear gunner reported that the formation's bombs were seen to hit the docks and shipping.

As soon as we were clear of the target I could feel that my aircraft had sustained some damage, but had no time to check as we were immediately attacked by three fighters – an ME109, a ME110[1] and an Italian Macchi 200. My fighter direction officer, Flight Lieutenant Dalton, was already in the astro-dome, letting me know the direction each fighter was attacking from. They were all quarter or stern attacks. With the running commentary from Dalton I took appropriate action to counter their attacks, but we still got a terrible hammering. I could hear bullets and cannon shells smashing their way down the fuselage and one or two of the cannon shells smashed into the armour plating behind my back. I could also see pieces of the port engine being shot off. Flight

---

[1] The official report said it was a JU 88 but I think it was a ME 110.

Lieutenant Dalton did a magnificent job keeping me informed of the fighter's movements.

I had headed north out to sea, as I knew the fighters had only about 20-30 minutes endurance before having to return to base to re-fuel. The formation had been broken up in the intense barrage and the others were nowhere to be seen. After some 15-20 minutes of running battle the fighters pulled away, which was just as well, as my rear gunner's guns had jammed and his turret was out of action as well as his intercom. My second pilot was wounded.

As soon as the enemy planes had left, my crew reported that our starboard outer engine was on fire and streaming smoke and flame behind, so I put the nose down and dived for the sea after operating the fire extinguisher on that engine. This was one method of putting out engine fires, and on this occasion it worked. I pulled out of the screaming dive at 500 feet over the sea, thankful that the excessive speed hadn't pulled the wings off and happily the fire was out. My port inner was giving only half power so I had only 2½ good engines to fly the 1,000 mile journey back. I lightened the aircraft by throwing out everything of weight that could be spared and finally, after some 7 hours, staggered back to Fayid in bright moonlight. I landed safely but the nose-wheel had been damaged and collapsed, causing my aircraft to slew off the runway on its nose in a cloud of sand until we finally stopped just short of a stone building.

Next day I viewed the aircraft and it looked like a sieve, with over 100 jagged holes. That mission to Benghazi was my worst in terms of being within a hair's breadth of being shot down.

People have asked me if I felt fear on these occasions and my answer is no. Apprehension and anxiety, yes in plenty, but fear, no.

In the middle of the onslaught by fighters, when I saw chunks of metal coming off my engines, the only feeling I had was as if an extremely sharp knife was being drawn slowly across my throat, just cutting the skin. Aerial combat is short-lived barely 15-20 minutes of intense activity before it was all over.

My longest mission was to Italy and back, to attack shipping at the Naval Base at Taranto. On leaving the target I discovered that I was losing fuel and one engine's oil pressure was dropping badly. I shut that engine down and landed on three engines at Sidi Barrani. I knew the Afrika Korps under Field Marshal Rommel was steadily attacking the British Eighth Army eastwards towards Cairo, but I was unaware exactly where he had got to. Desert warfare was fluid, so imagine how I felt when I arrived at RAF Sidi Barrani to be informed that our Army was withdrawing back and the Afrika Korps was only 12 miles away and expected to advance at any moment. I spent the night in a trench covered with a tent, in the congenial company of RAF fighter pilots – Spitfires, Hurricanes and Tomahawks (USA). I had the finest steak I ever ate in my life in their mess and was glad these young men got the best food – they deserved it!

The next day there was a terrific sandstorm and everyone went to ground and covered up. The sky was obliterated and sand got into everything. Even one's teeth got gritty, let alone one's hair and clothing. Next day every unit was packing up, the sky was blue again and the sun hot as usual. I managed to scrounge some petrol and had a hairy take-off. The Blenheim light twin-engine bombers had been sent off to attack the Afrika Korps. Some had crash-landed on return and were burning on the airfield, which was all sand and very stony, and I had to take off on three engines round them and just managed to get off safely and return to base.

As Rommel advanced to Alamein we had to fly up to Palestine (Israel) to an RAF aerodrome called St Jean, just north of Haifa, as the fighter squadrons were pushed back to Fayid, our old base in Egypt. St Jean airport was completely empty but all the facilities were there – officers and NCOs messes, ablution blocks, sleeping quarters, etc – all well built stone and tiled buildings, which we just took over. There was no furniture until our ground staff brought in trestle tables and we used bomb cases cut down for bar stools and chairs. The ingenuity of members of our squadron knew no bounds!

We were now further away from our targets, so on the long-haul missions we had to take off early at daybreak fly to Cairo for re-fuelling and take off again to complete our missions. Waiting to refuel and take off was hell. Our cockpits were like greenhouses in the hot sun. In our flying gear we were boiling and it was such a relief to get airborne.

Rommel and his Afrika Korps were finally held up at El Alamein and General Montgomery was put in charge of the 8th Army. We were fully stretched, with sorties almost every night or day, with maximum effort. The strain told on the aircrew. On one sortie when the aircrew were up at 4am, ready to take off, one aircraft was a few minutes late getting into place and our CO climbed up into the flight deck and gave the Flight Lieutenant pilot a right roasting in front of his crew. This went down really badly with the squadron. Aircrew were all volunteers, not conscripted men, and before the war most had been professional men or highly skilled artisans.

The next day I was approached by the squadron and, because I got on quite well with the CO, was asked to explain that his treatment of aircrew was considered unacceptable. We had been operating at full stretch for nearly six months in difficult circumstances and intensely hot weather, moving from base to base. We were like a large family.

Although I was most embarrassed, I managed to nail the CO in his tent and, as diplomatically as I could, I informed him of the feeling in the squadron. He was one of the old school RAF officers, about 10 years older than me, and I was his Squadron Leader Flight Commander, junior to him in rank. For a good five minutes I watched his face and saw him wrestling with his thoughts, which flitted across his features. He had been trained in strict pre-war discipline and had not taken account of the fact that this was a peoples' war and the old ways were out of date. I had visions of him having me court-martialled for insolence and lack of discipline for daring to confront him in this manner. His face was ashen when he looked up and it was evident to me that he realised that to lose his temper in front of a pilot's crew just as they were about to go on a mission was simply "not on".

He was a sincere and honest CO and I liked him and to give him credit he said it was difficult for a leopard to change his spots but he had got the message and would endeavour to improve matters – so in the end all was well. For the rest of his stay with the squadron he kept his word and gained much respect from the squadron as a result.

Tobruk had fallen to German forces at the end of June and was duly added to our list of targets. I was detailed to attack it on one of my daylight sorties, leading a formation of six Liberators at dusk, and managed to score a direct hit on Rommel's fuel dump. For a long time as we were on our way back to base my rear gunner reported that there was a raging fire 'down there' with a black pall of smoke billowing up to 15,000 feet visible for over 40 miles at our height. Subsequently I received a personal telegram from Air Vice Marshal Ritchie, Officer Commanding 205 Group, for being responsible for destroying 250,000 gallons of fuel that Rommel and his Afrika Korps badly needed for his tanks and army in the field. Tobruk was heavily defended and we received a fair amount of damage over the target, as well as being attacked briefly by a night fighter on the way back to base.

Shortly after this we moved again to RAF Aqir, between Tel Aviv and Haifa, whose CO was Group Captain Denny, who I had served under at Heliopolis, Egypt in 1937. He was a dapper little man, rather strait-laced and lacking in humour. At that station we had Australian ground crew to service our Liberators and they were doing a good job. We had some heavy thunderstorms and the tents these Aussies were living in were almost washed away. They had to service our aircraft out in the open in the heat and under these conditions they became bolshie and there was another near mutiny. Denny, like our old CO, was a bit of a martinet and insisted on King's regulations being observed at all times, even in the middle of the war when all were doing their best. The Aussies didn't take too kindly to this type of bullshit. Denny got huffy, but backed down in the end and left them alone. Like the sailors at Gibraltar, when service personnel are under great pressure and their part of the war was not going too well, being well-trained and discipline in their particular jobs, British servicemen and women are best left alone to get on with their job.

During the whole time I was in Egypt, I only had two days off from operations. I had a 15-cwt Ford truck for taking aircrew out to their aircraft and as a Flight Commander I made use of it and went to the French Club in Ismalia, on the Suez Canal, for lunch.

On coming out I couldn't believe it – my vehicle had vanished, although I had taken every precaution.

The second time I went there to do some shopping and have a decent meal, I parked my replacement Ford 15-cwt truck outside RAF 205 Group HQ for safety. Again I simply couldn't believe it when it had vanished – I even felt the bare road in disbelief. I reported it to the Army Police and they told me that the Army had recently gone up to take Lebanon and it was very likely that some overworked movement officer had seen my vehicle parked close to one of their conveys going up north and had detailed a driver to get it going to join up "and be quick about it". Perhaps it is still there giving good service in Beirut as a vintage vehicle.

On another occasion I was again lucky to escape with my life. As duty officer I was seeing the Squadron off on a sortie and was standing near the end of the runway to wave them off. It's a wonderful sight to see a whole squadron of 4-engine bombers take off one after the other in quick succession. I can never get tired of seeing aircraft take off and land, to me it's a real thrill, but not at this particular time because one of the aircraft's bombs started dropping off three quarters of the way down the runway, when the plane was almost airborne at 90 mph. Owing to the shape of bombs they run straight for a short distance and then zoom off to port or starboard (left or right) in a zigzag way. My first thought was to run but in a split second I realised that I might run into their path so stayed frozen while large bombs hurtled past me, some one way and some the other. One came so near I felt the wind as it passed. I had never known bombs to drop off in this fashion and it was so very unusual to have this experience – and survive.

Again I was duty officer on a very dark night when one of our aircraft returned with a wounded air gunner who was bleeding from being shot in the thigh. I had him put next to me in my truck to take him to the station MO and set off at speed to do my life-saving gallant job of getting him seen to in the shortest time. But the best of intentions sometimes go wrong. We had only moved to Aqir the day before and I realised I hadn't the faintest idea where sick quarters was located.

I became frantic with worry for the poor chap as he slumped, moaning, by my side as I careered round typically narrow RAF camp roads with whitewashed curbs in the middle of the night at great speed with dimmed headlights in a totally blacked-out camp. It was only a matter of luck that I came across sick quarters by accident after 10 minutes; it could have taken hours otherwise. Fortunately, the patient was all right after this somewhat hairy episode, so my 'white knight' act didn't go badly wrong.

Palestine is a lovely place; green in cultivated parts but bare and stony in the hills. We enjoyed dropping in to have a quick sea bathe at Nahariyya, a Jewish seaside resort with a fine sandy beach and the luxury (for the first time for me, even in 1942) of fresh water showers on the beach. The country is steeped in history; along the coast there was even a Roman aqueduct still working. It was the first time I ever saw grapefruit growing, right next to the aircraft parking bays where ground engineers worked on our engines adjacent to the citrus groves.

159 Squadron India January 3rd 1942

...I wish to say, dear, how silly I have been in my last few letters to you and I daresay you will have noticed how dis-

jointed they have been combined with a number of moans and general whining of discontent.

Well, Budge darling I wish to say how sorry I am that I have put any note of moaning in my letters to you – I feel better now that Xmas and the New Year are over because it was the memories of this period in previous years that made me break down because I missed you so much.

I realise now that I am out here for a very serious purpose and also a very good purpose and that is – to smash the Japs so that you and Penelope can live in peace. I realise it is highly unpleasant being away from you and home but until such time as it pleases God to have me sent home then it is very wrong of me to moan to you in my letters and thereby upsetting you and making you more miserable.

In all your letters to me you have shown me your fine character, Budge dear, in that you have never whined or said anything discouraging to me, only just cheerful news about you and our lovely Penelope, which of course I just love to hear all about.

God bless you for it.

242 Wing M.E.F. 26.01.42

...I am so looking forward to the photos of you and Penelope – hope they arrive here soon before I leave for our original destination in which will be in about one week from now. Please don't worry if you do not receive any mail for a bit as it will take some time to get through. I will write again, of course, before I leave, Dear.

You may be hearing me over the BBC some day soon and also reading of our exploits in the "Evening Standard". We made a recording of one trip for a possible BBC broadcast and also on one occasion took an Evening Standard Foreign Correspondent up on an ops trip recently.

He said he was going to write it up and send it home. I gave him your address so they may notify you.

I have been keeping very fit recently sweetheart and I am glad to hear that you and Penelope are well also. I'm due to play another game of soccer on Wednesday!! Poor old bones.

159 Squadron stayed in the Middle East until early November 1942 and then received orders to move again to their original destination in the India/Burma theatre of war. The RAF Strategic Air Force, of which we were part, had pounded away at the Afrika Corp's supply line for six months to great effect, in addition to the work of the RAF Desert Air Force, which worked directly with the Eighth Army. By 2nd September Rommel had only enough petrol for his tanks and vehicles to travel 60 miles and only half his supplies from Italy were reaching him before the decisive Allied victory at El Alamein under General Montgomery. We had flown out from the UK with two crews to each aircraft from 159 and 160 Squadrons. After Alamein 160 Squadron, who had received their full complement of aircraft by that time, continued their bombing programme with the Eighth Army through to Tunis and Italy.

Thus we were free to proceed to India in our own time.

242 Wing M.E.F. 30th October 1942

...I too hate the thought of going in the opposite direction and I've done my best to stop it but it wouldn't work – being a key man in the squadron doesn't help any. I want you darling to have great courage and go about your normal duties and

looking after Penelope and writing to me. I am doing the same and am thinking about you so much at all sorts of odd times during the day. It is a great gap in our lives this being parted so long but we have so many blessings haven't we – 1. Penelope, 2. Complete trust, love and understanding between us 3. A roof over our heads and food in our mouths.

For my part sweet, I shall not rest in my endeavours to return to England though at the same time I shall plod on to the best of my ability until providence sees fit to let me return.

RAF Sabkani Imara November 19*th* 1942

...At the moment I write by the light of my pressure kerosene lamp (made in Germany)- outside it is dark (7pm) and the warm air is full of the noise of my lamp and the eternal crickets.

When I first arrived here the locals had a feast week which happens practically every two weeks and all day and all night I could hear the pom–pom–pom of the village drums – just like a ruddy film in which Dorothy Lamour might feature.

Today was bright and cheerful – I had been up 'til 2 am being "OC" Night flying and did not rise 'til 9 am. There was not a cloud in the sky and I felt lazy...During the afternoon the flight indulged in a little fishing – Bamboo poles and cotton thread with local worms and hooks supplied the sport on a small lake at the back of the flight office. The fish are only 1½ inches long – but anything for a change.

I took off from Aqir at the end of November '42 and flew down the Persian Gulf, the coast of Iran and Baluchistan to Karachi (now in Pakistan), a distance of over 2,000 miles – a long night flight.

Once more I was lucky, as I could so easily have lost my life. Arriving early in the morning I made the usual approach and put my undercarriage down, only to find that my starboard undercarriage had stuck halfway down (the ram that forced the wheels down had snapped). I sized up the situation and decided to attempt to land the aircraft in order to save as much of it as possible but I gave the crew the option to stay or parachute to safety. All but my co-pilot, F/O Evans duly departed and landed safely. I thought Evans very brave to opt to stay with me and I was grateful for his support. I flew around to use up as much fuel as possible, to lessen the possibility of fire, made my normal approach as slow as I could, just above stalling speed, and touched down quite normally on the sandy surface. I was half way across the airfield when slowly the starboard wing dropped and the outer engine dug into the ground. The plane shook and shuddered and ground looped about 45 degrees before coming to rest in a huge cloud of dust and stones.

I anticipated it would flame immediately with the hot engines so I was out of the escape hatch in 2/5^{ths} of a second along with my co-pilot and running like hell. Fortunately, it did not catch fire but was a write-off, the frame being badly twisted. A day or two later, after making my report, I picked up another Liberator and flew another 1,500 miles across to Salboni RAF airfield, about 60 miles west of Calcutta. My arrival coincided with the tail end of a hurricane that had devastated the area south of us along the coast around Orissa. Thousands of local Indians had been killed in the floods and terrific winds and it seemed to us that numerous vultures around could hardly get off the ground, they were so full of animal and human flesh. For a few days we walked at about 45 degrees to the wind to keep on our feet, the temperature was in the 100's and perspiration poured from us day and night. We could never get dry.

November 15th 1942 R.A.F. Salbani India

...about two weeks ago – before I arrived they had a typhoon here – lots of trees were blown down, just torn out by their roots. All the roads were blocked the Indians near the coast were overwhelmed by a tidal wave as you probably read in the papers.

The country round about is like paradise after Egypt and Palestine. Everything is green. It is wild flat country with many forests and lakes and rivers. The place abounds with wonderful bird life (birds of every colour) and you would be amazed at the beauty of the butterflies – some are as large as sparrows. I hope to have a spot of shooting. We live in thatched roof huts with brick walls and a veranda. Outside are bamboo clumps and tall trees. Several small squirrels (tree rats) and 4 or 5 Indian crows bid me good morning when I awaken. There is no glass in the windows, only wooden shutters. The weather is glorious – cool at night (2 blankets) and fresh in the early morning – Its is usually rather hot in the middle of the day. When there is rain about – it is muggy close and sticky.

18th November 1942

...well my sweetheart – I shall miss you beyond words this Christmas – I shall miss your exhilarating excitement which you imparted to me before you are allowed to open your parcels – by me. I miss your companionship most of all – your

gay spirit, your laughter and that of our beloved daughter Penelope. I kiss you at night when we have quiet talks on the days happenings – I miss your cooking and the way you welcomed me home every evening, I even miss your few faults...all these made up my life which is so barren and different now – as I have said in former letters Budge darling – I am just existing now and the time I am away from you is just as much wasted time. I feel pretty fed up but can do nothing about it so must do what I know you would advise that is – do my job well and hope for the best...

...tell Penelope all about me and please send as many photos as possible – I've got to go now Sweet to get out a night flying programme.

17th December 1942 159 Sqn RAF India (Letter No.50)

...It doesn't seem like Christmas here with the sun shining strongly in the middle of the day. Its cold in the mornings, evenings and at night so we are wearing Blue. I have shaved off my moustachios which got huge but have decided to grow an even bigger one!!

I am doing a temporary job as admin officer while the position is awaiting to be filled and as President of the Service institute (for the Airmen) I am off to Calcutta to see about supplies and extras for their Xmas dinner. Wish I were doing it for my own family instead. I've such a large family now though and all boys!!

159 Squadron RAF India 3rd January 1943

...On Christmas Eve all the officers attended a Concert party given by the airmen in the squn. The stage was closed on three sides. The 3rd opening to the audience who sat in the open. There is no roof and everything was home made including the "crooners" microphone and loudspeaker.

It was quite good – there was a minstrel band of mouth organs, banjo and ukulele. One pianist who played simply magnificently on a dreadful old piano bought from Calcutta. A few sketches and cockney backchat Comedians interspersed with some hearty community singing of popular numbers. There were of course quite a number of veiled references about the W/c and S/l's. On the whole it was quite good considering the difficulties under which the performers worked.

On Christmas morning at 1000 hrs the officers played soccer against the senior sgts, all in fancy dress so that the men can have a good laugh. There were many funny costumes including that of the W/c who wore a high collar with red bow tie, no shirt, and his bearers baggy white trousers (muslin)

I have taken a number of colour cine pictures of the game which I hope to be able to show you later.

At midday the officers served the airmen Xmas dinner, an old custom which has been in practice since the last 14 –18 war.

At night we had a proper "dinner" night – all in blue uniform with candles, passing the port and "The King" etc after which speeches were made all round. This continued into a pretty good party which went far into the night.

I operated on Boxing Day – just a nice reminder that Xmas festivities were not the most important items on the programme.

Since then I have been doing very little. Max is on a 48 hour pass to Calcutta and so I am busy with the flight.

In the evenings, about one hour before sundown, I usually take a brisk walk into the surrounding bush country with my shotgun to try and bag a dove or pigeon. Both make excellent savouries after dinner. There are also some jungle fowl (rather like pheasant) and hyena. I have not shot any of the latter yet.

Many of the birds have beautiful colourings. The blue jays have brilliant shades of blue wings, the fly catchers are of all bright colours and are incredibly quick in the air as you can imagine they would be to catch flies. The most common birds are the old familiar Indian crow with a grey head. Perhaps next comes the hawk with it marvellous orange back and wings and super gliding qualities.

Then there is the large, ugly ungainly vulture with its long scraggy neck. They are about as big as a large turkey and no-one is allowed to shoot them (Fine 5) because they are scavengers.

As soon as we had our full compliment of aircraft we started operating on long distance targets. Here the climate and terrain was quite different from the dry, sandy Middle East. We had tarmac runways on hard-core on which worked local labour, including many women, who fetched stones in baskets on their heads. Some were pregnant and it was quite common for one of these to have her baby at the side of the runway, having worked right up to her time. She generally spent only a short time before getting up herself and walking off.

Vultures and similar large birds were a danger to airborne aircraft flying low, as they could smash the cockpit windscreen or damage an engine badly by flying into it. They were heavy birds!

We were quite comfortable as we lived in newly-built huts besides the mess. The officers' mess was a large, whitewashed building with lounge-cum-bar and a dining room with kitchen behind. It was not long before a reasonable English garden was in bloom along the front and sides to make us feel at home. The heat was excessive, so we had a proper *punkah* system with a resident *punkah-wallah* to work it. We asked him one day if he would like a trip in one of our Liberators but he declined saying, "birds fly by day but only unwise people fly by night." I am sure he meant "idiots" but was being polite! A worthy answer from a local man of the soil.

It was here that I got a taste for pink gin with pearl onions. Some of the whiskies and gins made in India were first class but there was a lot of hooch around, which was fearsome stuff, resulting in some pretty rough party nights in the mess when we were stood down through bad weather. Outside my room, the builder put a raised cement circle with my name S/Ldr J.L. Beck DFC, which is probably still there today.

I mentioned that some of our pilots had produced a nice garden with the help of their bearers (we each had one) but one day some local Bengali cows got in and began to eat the much-cosseted plants and were still at it when our botanically-minded pilots came out to view their precious garden. There was, of course, a lot of cursing and someone started throwing stones to frighten them off. One rather large stone hit a cow on the head, which promptly gave up further thoughts of living and fell down dead. This happened just after breakfast and, believe it or not, the next day by 10am all that was left of that animal was a whitened skeleton. Nature's scavengers worked overtime in these parts, it seemed.

It's funny how these little incidents stick in one's mind permanently, even after half a century. Another two examples come to mind. I had brought out from the UK a shortened 12 bore shotgun and had managed to bag some snipe in the paddy fields round about, Bengal being a rice-growing area. We had enough for dinner one night and after a nice few rounds of pink gins we went into dinner, already savouring the snipe in our minds. We all set to with gusto, until one officer opened his and a frog sprang out. Obviously underdone! Several diners went a bit green and fled the table.

At that time our food was not good. We had to live on dried potatoes, skinned tomatoes, curried eggs and Aussie butter that came in tins and tasted like axle grease. Soya sausages were not much better. The Indians in that region fared worse. There was a famine, owing to failure of the rice crop, but they couldn't eat our grub, even when offered. Some were even throwing themselves in front of trains rather than starve. Anything can happen out in these places, which are out of the ordinary for us westerners. One night I was called out on a pitch-black night when a fire was reported on our aerodrome. I rushed out, only to find a funeral pyre of logs burning away merrily, just off a runway, being witnessed by a group of locals who were burning the corpse of an old man, sitting on top in a chair. No harm done, just a local custom, so I let it finish and the mourners departed back home.

RAF India Command 7th February 1943

...I am working very hard dearest as the C.O. is on 14 days leave and Max Boffee is down with malaria. I am now

running the Sqn on my own with only F/LT. to help and operating at the same time!! Have not been outside the camp for three weeks what price having a good time eh? B- awful really my sweet the flt work is getting monotonous . Same faces day in – day out you know.

Max is a lucky devil – believe he is to get a W/C job at Command Delhi – best for me as no promotion while he is here in squadron as he is my senior.

RAF Indian Command 14th February 1943

Our Own Sweet baby daughter – Penelope Mary Ann Beck,

Your Daddy had such a terrible thought this evening – had he written to wish you "Many Happy Returns" of your 2nd Birthday?

He was sure he had written about the end of January but as there was just a wee bit of doubt in the back of his mind he has decided to write to you again just in case.

Well Penelope – I do so hope you will have such a happy birthday – Mummy, I am sure, has lots of nice things both to try on, smell, and eat which little girls just love to have. Your Mummy is such a clever girl at picking out just the right sort of presents.

It will not be difficult for your Daddy (who is terribly homesick) to imagine what your second birthday will be like. He thinks it will probably run something like this:- A small rosy cheeked babe will wake up with wide sparkling eyes – so ex-cited!! A pattering of little feet across the room and then up – bounce and into mummy's bed (lucky little girl!)

Shrieks of "wake up Mummy" where are my presents I must open them now (just like her dear Mummy) Lots of lovely presents will be taken out from lots of crackly brown and coloured paper wrappings. Shrieks of delight and a flood of kisses. After breakfast a lot of dressing up for a nice long walk with mummy and auntie Joan and Vera and Grand-mama. Perhaps a little stop to say hello to Grand-mama down the street. Grand-papa will say "There, there little thing"

Then an enormous lunch followed by an exciting tea party with lots of coloured cakes and friendly little people to play with. Perhaps sit up later than usual to a radio programme before a tired happy little soul will fall fast asleep...

Our targets and sphere of operations were now over Burma. The terrain was inhospitable in that we had to fly over the Chin or Naga mountain range which ran north to south, all covered with dense teak forests, or over the sea in the Bay of Bengal, leading to the Burmese capital of Rangoon in the south over the Chindwin and Irrawaddy rivers. Beyond that was the Shan mountain range. Forced landings were largely out of the question, as the choice was forest, paddy fields or the sea. Our targets were airfields, supply dumps, railway marshalling yards, communications, bridges and enemy troop concentrations, along with general reconnaissance.

The weather took its toll during monsoon conditions and at one time either due to enemy action or lack of maintenance due to heat and weather we were down to three serviceable aircraft for operations. This situation improved rapidly in better weather and the receipt of replacements. During the latter part of my second tour, due to shortage of aircraft, I would take over any aircraft in my flight (as Flight Commander) so that I could observe the efficiency of my pilots and crews. This procedure encouraged them and enabled me to know them better.

Our flights of long duration took us into horrific tropical storms and we lost several crews either through enemy action or storms. One night I was duty CO of operations and our CO, Wing Commander Skinner, was lost over Rangoon, believed shot down by a Jap night fighter. We waited and waited for his return but he and his crew were never seen again, though after the war when I came to Jersey I heard a rumour that he and the crew were captured and executed, but I have no proof of this.

In our camp, of course, all was gloom. His bearer, together with other bearers, held a vigil and service of some sort outside his room for a number of nights. We thought this was very touching to honour him in this way, as we were pretty well hardened to this experience, which had happened all the time on ops in the UK, Egypt and now India/Burma. I was personally affected, as I knew him best out of our squadron. He was a good CO, despite the hiccup in Palestine. His place was taken by Max Boffee, our senior Flight Commander, who was promoted to Wing Commander of 159 Squadron.

Shortly after this episode I was picked to fly back to England, taking with me the Viceroy of India, Field Marshal Wavell and the RAF C-in-C India, Air Marshal Sir Richard Peirce. I met them at Karachi for tea when my Liberator (its bomb bay converted for passenger comfort) was standing on the apron outside. I was introduced and chatted for a short while about the long journey ahead when my flight sergeant came in, saluted me and by signs indicated he wanted a word with me outside. But I was busy conversing with my VIPs and could not get away immediately. My flight sergeant finally tugged at my sleeve rather urgently, so I excused myself and went outside. He was very agitated and took me over to my Liberator, where I saw the cause of his worry. All along the underside of one wing, petrol was dripping from the rivets. I was absolutely appalled and shocked to find that at this late hour my journey had to be scrubbed. As a result, the VIPs went on to Cairo by Dakota and I was instructed to follow with a serviceable aircraft to pick them up for the final flight to England.

My replacement Liberator arrived the following day and we took off in the evening for Cairo. I got as far as the Persian Gulf but had to land at RAF Sharja, on the coast just inside the Gulf in the United Arab Emirates, with loss of oil pressure on one engine. As soon as I had fixed up a guard on my aircraft we were all herded into a small stone-built fort, reminiscent of the forts of the French Foreign Legion in Morocco in the 1930s film *Beau Geste*. It was explained to us that marauding Bedouin tribesmen would take pot-shots at anyone they found in the desert at night in the dark. Next morning I had a sea bathe, which was wonderful, as it was so very hot. A curious phenomenon was that the salty sea appeared warmer than the air on coming out.

Alas, my journey to England was cancelled, as my VIPs were due for a conference in Whitehall and my engine could not be put right in time. I had so looked forward to seeing Budge in the middle of my overseas tour, even if only for a few hours, but on the other hand, if my wing tanks had leaked while I was flying north near the middle of the Atlantic, I would surely have run out of fuel and have had to flop down in the ocean, with little hope of surviving a sea landing or being rescue hundreds of miles from land in the middle of a war. Flying routes over Europe were, of course, completely out, as Europe was occupied by the Axis powers.

Somewhat deflated, I returned to my Flight Commander duties with 159 Squadron.

RAF Station Habbanyah Iraq Easter Sunday 1943

...I have sent no letter to you since the 11th April because on that date I was most happily informed that I was to take an aircraft back to the U.K. on a ferrying flight. My darling you can only guess how I felt! That meant Easter with my beloved ones. I thought that there would be no need to write as I hoped to present myself in person. On the very next day I shot off from my station on the long flight home – sweetheart I've had such disappointments since – twice my aircraft have failed me and I'm stuck here- about halfway.

Up to the present I still have orders to proceed home when another aircraft arrives but I thought that if the whole thing is cancelled then I must not let the gap in my correspondence widen too far so I am now writing just in case so you will know what happened. I sent you a wire on the 14th April to let you know I was coming – I keep hoping and praying I shall still make it as I so much want to see you if only for a few hours or a few days leave before unhappily I shall have to return. It means so much, this break for us after so long a parting.

RAF Habbanyay, Iraq 29th April '43

Now that I have calmed down a little I will write you the whole sad story which brings me to the above station. I was so upset that I simple could not write yesterday.

Here is my story, calmly and dispassionately: On the 11th Max told me that an a/c was wanted for an important ferry job to the U.K. and that I could go. Believe me darling I was leaping for joy at the thought of being able to see my dearly beloved wife and sweetheart baby daughter once again after years of absence.

I took off on the 12th from my unit and spent a week at the dispatching base, waiting for my a/c to be fitted with special fittings. Then on the 18th I was ready to go. 30 minutes before I was due off I had a bad petrol leak from the a/c. Well my darling – my passengers went on ahead- I was to catch them up halfway home when I'd had new petrol tanks put in. For 3 days the engineers worked on my a/c but they couldn't fix it, then another a/c was dispatched from my squadron for me to take on instead. I left the dispatching base in the second a/c on 22nd for my first stopping place en route for home. Then goddam everything I had two engines cutting in the air. I had a night landing at this station and on coming to rest safely I discovered I had a bad oil leak in one engine and ignition trouble in another.

The oil leak necessitated a complete engine change and there were no facilities on this station and no spare engine.

I then had instructions to wait a couple of days for my original a/c which should be ready by then. I waited until yesterday my darling, then an a/c from another squadron came through on the same mission en route for the U.K. with a complete crew.

I have had no further instructions since. I expect to be re-called any moment ...

It has been one of the greatest disappointments of my life Budge darling and at the present everything seems pretty flat. However if I can't overcome these set backs in a manly fashion and have courage to face facts I wouldn't be worthy of being your husband.

I'm going to think of this episode as being damned hard luck and I <u>will</u> not let it get me down..

Sharjah (Red Sea) Persian Gulf. 3ʳᵈ May 1943

...here's a short letter to tell you of my further adventures

...I left Habbinyah yesterday because my a/c was still u/s and will take weeks to put right. My spare pilot is bringing it back. I had a comfortable ride here in a D.C. passenger plane en route for India. We refuelled and had only just taken off when we had engine trouble. My my Budge the trouble I've had in the last few weeks is incredible. So now we have to stay here for the engine to be put right. Two days I expect.

The place is a real desert station. Very small and I am staying in an unbelievable place. Just like the films of Beau Geste – in an old square fort !! still in use. You can walk round the walls on a broad path, well protected by a breastwork for shooting over.

The native Arabian Arabs (nomads) sometimes get a bit excited and pop off a few rounds.

There is no communication with the outside world except by plane or sea. There is nothing here except a dirty Wog village on the sea shore, and a few palm trees – otherwise desert and rugged bare hills.

First Staff Appointment – Overseas Training Station

I found my seven months in Bengal most interesting. Our aerodrome was situated on level countryside near the foothills of the central plateau to the west and to the east was the 300 mile

River Delta through which the Rivers Ganges and the Brahmapu-tra flowed on their way, fanning out to the tiger and crocodile infested multiple creeks of the Sundarbans in the Bay of Bengal.

By April 1943 I had been on two tours of operations – one against Nazi Germany 1940/41 over Europe and the second over the Middle East against the Axis powers of Germany and Italy in Libya and the Mediterranean generally, followed by the comple-tion of my second tour over Burma against the third Axis power – Japan. I had been awarded a DFC in both campaign theatres of war, with a mention in dispatches in the Middle East. I was then taken off operations with 159 Squadron and posted as Station Commander to RAF Poona (Pune), a newly-constructed aerodrome close to Kirkee Arsenal (Army) in British Army Southern Command area. Poona was in the Western Ghats, on a plateau of mountainous country about 100 miles inland from the coastal plain and Bombay. The climate was moderated by being up on an escarpment near the top of the plateau and was classed as a 'semi-hill station' in colonial days.

It was over 1,000 miles from the front from which I had just come and was being developed as an aircrew transit pool to take fresh aircrews arriving from England. My job was to acclimatise them to India, give them refresher courses in their particular field and keep them in flying experience. For this, my instructor flights had Harvards and Hurricanes. The aerodrome consisted of a single strip of conventional length, with a headquarters building for admin and buildings for two flights. When I arrived, the strip had only just been completed and there was a massive labour force dotted all over the place in makeshift camps. There was no boundary fence, although at the entrance guardroom, there was a balance pole barrier, which was raised to allow entry by vehicles. It was the subject of much mirth, as there was nothing to indicate a boundary on either side of it and anyone could just walk round this contraption at will. There was the usual Airmen's and Sergeants' messes and the officers were quartered in a pleasant three-storey house on the outskirts of the British Cantonment in Poona.

I had no experience of running an RAF station but in the usual casual service way I rolled up my sleeves, as the saying goes, and got down to this entirely new job of management. My experience at Ardingly in running sporting events, the OTC and my last appointments as Flight Commander of a heavy four engined bomber squadron helped me a great deal in getting started and the one thing I learnt very quickly was the art of delegation. In a short time, as soon as the huts were constructed, I had picked my instructor team to keep aircrew in training and I was lucky in my choice. They had all had battle experience in their category – navigation, gunnery, radio communication and general airmanship. They were a good bunch who kept the intakes on top of their skills as aircrew while waiting to be posted as replacements to the various squadrons operating at the front.

Getting the whole show going was an exacting job. A new control tower overlooking the runway was not finished – it had to be rebuilt because the original specification indicated that it had to be well camouflaged and the local construction company had taken this instruction far too literally. I was astonished to find that the original one had already been built – around an enormous tree. Although well nigh impossible to spot from the air, it was much too far away from the runway, which was barely visible from the roof when peering through the foliage – quite useless for controlling aircraft movements.

~ *Chocks Away!* ~

RAF Indian Command Sunday 30ᵗʰ May '43

...I have had a hell of a time the last few days and I still don't know whether I stand on my arse or my elbow (excuse pliss the crude language)

I am now C.O. of a training unit. I cannot tell you exactly what kind of unit it is or where but I can say that I already have a large number of pupils thrust on the unit and as yet there is absolutely no organisation!! By that I mean we have only about half our establishment of men to do the work. No equipment, and no telephones or electric light. Our buildings are spread out over a large area as big as Bedford Park. And your poor unfortunate husband has got to get the whole station into running order. How its going to be done I don't know. My darling this is one of the times when I need you so very much I would feel so much better if I could discuss matters with you because you are often able to advise me well. Your companionship – the loss of which I feel so much – would help me no end at a time like this. Oh how I long to be back home with you.

Time will tell though my sweet how this new venture will turn out. The former C.O. has been suspended from his duties by the Air Officer Commanding the Group for not doing enough – I don't think the poor chap had a chance so how will I fare ? We shall see. Thank goodness I have those photos of you and Penelope to chat to just before going to sleep – you're such a comfort dear.

Poona is my nearest big town and is very pleasant though too full of Army officers. The monsoon is due within a week or so and every day sees more and more cloud hanging over the hills.

RAF Indian Command 13ᵗʰ June Sunday

...Today I was looking in my 1942 diary and on Tuesday 21ˢᵗ April I find an entry "Met Budge at Peterborough, she was "terribly pleased to see me cos she loves me so much" and it wasn't in my writing ! Believe me my sweet – that's an awful nice thing to say and I do appreciate it so terribly. Do you remember writing it ? You need never be afraid for me being out in a foreign country without you because this last year has brought home to me so powerfully the beauty of our union which is so much a part of my life. I am not being sentimental, darling, I am 30 years of age and have been through a great deal since I last saw your sweet self. Its just that I feel that way, automatically, without nonsense or anything.

Please forgive me for being so silly and writing it all down and covering half my letter when you want some news.

How do you like being the wife of a Wing Commander who was "mentioned in dispatches" last January ?

27ᵗʰ June 1943

...Darling I am not receiving your letters quite so frequently so I do hope none are getting lost in the post...I have not received anything in the last 12 days and feel so depressed as your letters mean such a lot ...I've been Wing Commander since 6ᵗʰ June, 21 days ago and it seems only yesterday. Time flies. I do hope you received my wire which was sent on first priority and cost a fortune so that I could be the first to tell you. The day before yesterday I received a signal from the Air

Office Commanding Bengal to congratulate me on the award
of a bar to my DFC. –By jingo Budge I do wish you could be
here so that I could feel proud and elated but as you are not
here to share this honour with me I have just had a drink or
two with the chaps and taken it very quietly

How is Penelope sweet? She is now 2 years 2 months old
and we shall soon be thinking of school for the darling. Do tell
me all she is doing. I starve for news of her daily life. ...

On one of my inspections round the far parts of the aerodrome
I found a small Buddhist chapel, built since my last inspection. It
was tiny and no way did it impede the working of the station. As I
approached, a Saffron-robed priest came out, a nice little man, and
I acquainted him of the fact that this was Air Ministry property
and enquired as to who had given him permission. After a
minute's contemplation he said, "the Lord Buddha". I weighed up
the situation, taking into account that we already had hundreds of
construction workers dotted about in various locations on site,
living with their families in makeshift tents, who might benefit
from his moral guidance, so I let him remain, with supervision
from the guardroom. Secretly, I comforted myself that the Lord
Buddha probably held the higher moral ground over the Air
Ministry!

During wartime, tragedies happened all the time. A civilian
aircraft maintenance unit used our runway and one morning a
Blenheim being air tested had just become airborne when it
turned completely over and crashed onto the aerodrome workers
camps, just at the time their midday meal was being prepared. It
burst into flames and cut a sward through the camp, killing all in
its path. There was nothing left. I read the report and it said that a

99 (Bomber) Squadron Coming of Age Dinner May Fair Hotel, London, December 17th 1938. Top Table (L to R) Mr. Handley-Page, W/Cdr HE Walker, Mr. L.A. Patterson, Air Cdre A.A. Thompson, Capt Sommers (F/O Beck right hand side, next to window).

The Author as Range Officer ~ watching 216 Squadron dropping
8½ lb practise bombs from 10,000 feet ~ October 1937.

The Author (centre, back row) and other members of 216 Squadron
in front of Vickers Valencia bomber transport ~ Cairo 1937.

'A' Flight, 99 Squadron RAF Mildenhall Suffolk 1938/9.

May 1939 ~ Author in Anson aircraft at Manston on Astro Course.

No.9 Astro Course 1939.

Flying Officer Beck marries Mary Broad ~ Seaford, Sussex ~ Friday 29th September 1939.

Two telegrams to arrange our wedding during just 24-hours leave.

Family wedding group ~ Seaford, Sussex ~ Friday 29th September 1939.

Just married ~ 1940.

Author with 214 Squadron at Stradishall, 1940.

214 Squadron ~ August 1940 ~ Author with crew of Wellington 'G' for George.

A commemorative Jersey a postage stamp featuring
the Author's 214 Squadron Wellington ~ G-BU N2776.

During a raid on marshalling yards at Osnabruck Germany, 'G' George was hit in three places by Flak.
Picture shows a large patch over damage to the fuselage, suitably marked Friday 13th 1940
(from *Portrait of a Bomber Pilot* the biography of Flt Lt Jack Wetherly DFC by Christopher Jary)

Photo of a Wellington with signatures of all 214 Squadron officers ~ 1940-41.

Vickers Wellington III bomber based at Mildenhall

The Author at the controls ~ 1941.

King George VI and Queen Elizabeth with Air Marshal Sir Richard Pierce (Commander-in-Chief, RAF Bomber Command) and Air Vice Marshal J. E. Baldwin Air Officer Commanding No.3 Group, photographed outside the officers mess at RAF Stradishall, Suffolk, February 1941.

Warnung

Großbritannien an das Deutsche Volk.

Deutsche,

Mit kühl erwogenem Vorsatz hat die Reichsregierung Großbritannien Krieg aufgezwungen. Wohl wußte sie, daß die Folgen ihrer Handlung die Menschheit in ein größeres Unheil stürzen, als 1914 es tat. Im April gab der Reichskanzler euch und der Welt die Versicherung seiner friedlichen Absichten; sie erwies sich als ebenso wertlos wie seine im September des Vorjahres im Sportpalast verkündeten Worte: „Wir haben keine weiteren territorialen Forderungen in Europa zu stellen."

Niemals hat eine Regierung ihre Untertanen unter geringerem Vorwand in den Tod geschickt. Dieser Krieg ist gänzlich unnötig. Von keiner Seite waren deutsches Land und deutsches Recht bedroht. Niemand verhinderte die Wiederbesetzung des Rheinlandes, den Vollzug des Anschlusses und die unblutig durchgeführte Einkörperung der Sudeten in das Reich. Weder wir, noch irgendein anderes Land, versuchte je dem Ausbau des deutschen Reiches Schranken zu setzen—solange dieses nicht die Unabhängigkeit nicht-deutscher Völker verletzte.

Allen Bestrebungen Deutschlands—solange sie Andern gerecht blieben—hätte man in friedlicher Beratung Rechnung getragen.

273

!!! Warnung !!!

— Seite 2 —

Präsident Roosevelt hat euch sowohl Frieden mit Ehren als auch die Aussicht auf materielle Wohlfahrt angeboten. An Stelle dessen hat eure Regierung euch zu dem Massenmord, dem Elend und den Entbehrungen eines Krieges verurteilt, den zu gewinnen sie nicht einmal erhoffen können.

Nicht uns, sondern euch haben sie betrogen. Durch Jahre hindurch hat euch eine eiserne Zensur Wahrheiten unterschlagen, die selbst unzivilisierten Völkern bekannt sind. Diese Zensur hält den Geist des deutschen Volkes in einem Konzentrationslager gefangen. Wie sonst konnten sie es wagen, die Zusammenarbeit friedliebender Völker zur Sicherung des Friedens fälschlich als feindliche Einkreisung darzustellen? Wir hegen keine Feindseligkeit gegen euch, das deutsche Volk.

Diese Nazi Zensur hat euch verheimlicht, daß ihr nicht über die Mittel verfügt, einen langen Krieg durchzuhalten. Trotz erdrückender Steuer laßt seid ihr am Rande des Bankrotts. Wir und unsere Bundesgenossen verfügen über unermeßliche Reserven an Mannestraft, Rüstung und Vorräten. Wir sind zu stark, durch Hiebe gebrochen zu werden und können euch unerbittlich bis zur Enderschöpfung bekämpfen.

Ihr, das deutsche Volk, habt das Recht, auf Frieden zu bestehen jetzt und zu jeder Zeit. Auch wir wünschen den Frieden und sind bereit, ihn mit jeder aufrichtig friedlich gesinnten deutschen Regierung abzuschließen.

Front and back of a British propaganda leaflet.

Many millions of similar leaflets were dropped over Germany by the RAF.

(Translated on following page.)

Warning
Great Britain to the German Nation

Germans,

With coldly calculated resolution the Reich Government has forced Great Britain to go to war. It was well aware that the consequences of its actions would plunge humanity into a greater disaster than 1914 did. In April the Reichskanzler gave you and the world the assurance of his peaceful intentions; **it turned out to be as worthless** as his words spoken in September of the previous year in the sports stadium: "We have no further territorial claims in Europe."

Never has a government sent its subjects to their deaths for a slighter excuse. This war is quite unnecessary. From no side were German territory and German law threatened. No-one prevented the reoccupation of the Rhineland, the completion of the *Anschluss* and the bloodless incorporation of the Sudeten into the Reich. Neither we nor any other country ever tried to put limits on the development of the German Reich – as long as this did not harm the independence of non-German nations.

All Germany's objectives – so long as they were not unjust towards others – could have been taken into account by peaceful consultation.

!!! Warning!!!
~ Page 2 ~

President Roosevelt has offered you both peace and honour and also the prospect of material prosperity. In place of that your government has **condemned you to mass murder, distress and the deprivations of a war** which they cannot hope to win.

They have deceived not us but you. For years on end an iron censorship has concealed the truths which are known to even uncivilized nations. This censorship is holding the **spirit** of the German nation captive in a **concentration camp.** How else could they dare to present the cooperation of peace-loving nations for safeguarding peace falsely as hostile isolation? We hold **no hostile feelings** towards you, the German nation.

This Nazi censorship has **hidden** from you the fact that you **do not have the means** to sustain a long war. Despite a crushing tax burden you are **on the edge of bankruptcy.** We and our allies have **immeasurable reserves of manpower, arms and supplies** at our disposal. We are too strong to be broken by blows and can fight you relentlessly to the bitter end.

You, the German nation, have the right to insist on peace now and at any time. We also want peace and are prepared to **make it with any sincere, peacefully-minded German government.**

Budge with baby Penelope ~ 1941

The Author with Penelope, just before leaving for overseas posting.

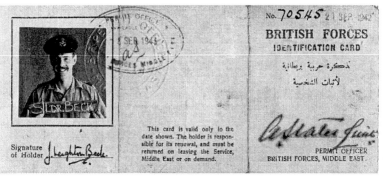

Front and back of the Author's British Forces identity card ~ Egypt 1942.

"Block" ~ Captain Ken Hay RA ~ and Author at Gibraltar ~ 2 June 1942.

159 Sqn RAF Liberator II of Allied Strategic Air Force in Egypt 1942 and 1943
in RAF Air Command South East Asia India/Burma.

B24 Liberator 159 Squadron Based at Fayid on the Bitter Lakes, Suez, Eqypt 1942. Carrying out maintenance on Upper Turret .303 Vickers Machine Guns.

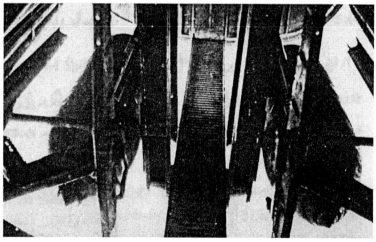

Egypt 1942 ~ Inside a 159 Sqn Liberator, showing bomb-bay, looking aft.
This bay linked the forepart of the aircraft (cockpit and Nav/Radio section) with the rear fuselage by means of a narrow (approx 10-inch) ribbed catwalk.

The Bomb doors are open (rolled up each side of the fuselage) and two bombs are in place. When the bomb doors were open at 20,000 feet, walking along the catwalk called for a lot of concentration!

B24 Liberator GR V1 of Coastal Command and 'B' Flight ~ Egypt 1942.

Sgt GRAHAM Sgt...KING... ...Sgt...WHINNEY Sgt KENT.
F/o MAJLIE S/L BELL.D.F.C. P/o TOOMAS. Sgt CARRIGAN.
Sgt NUTTRIDGE.

The Author, 'B' Flight commander with Liberator crew ~ Egypt 1942.

Telegrams home from India.

The Author with the rogue leopard shot near Poona at
the request of a local village headman ~ August 1943.

Aircrew Training Pool Officers Mess
Sethua House, Poona ~ November 1943.

Men of No.221 Group 3rd Tactical Air Force SEAC on parade ~ 1943.

The Author taking the salute as Officer Commanding.

Airmail Christmas card sent to Penelope ~ Christmas 1943.

Decorated in India

Wing Commander J. L. Beck, of Esmond-road, London, awarded the Bar to his D.F.C. in India.

Cutting from the *Evening Standard* Wednesday, October 13, 1943.

Congratulations from Budge following the
Author's award of bar to DFC ~ 1 July 1943.

Congratulations from SAC Poona on Air Force (India) form.

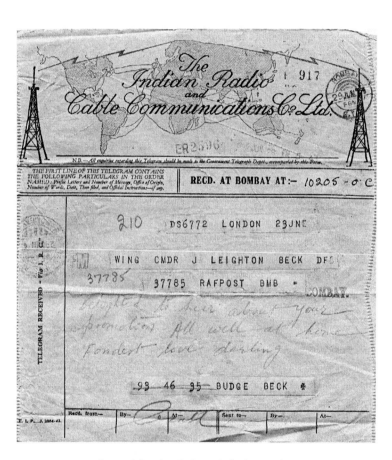

Congratulations from Budge on Author's promotion
to rank of Wing Commander ~ 29 June 1943.

From:- Air Commodore F.J. Vincent, C.B.E., D.F.C.

HEADQUARTERS 227 GROUP R. A. F.,
INDIA.

DO/FJV/319.

Dated 7th July 1943. 194 .

Dear Beck

I have just seen your name in Command Routine Orders and I am delighted to find that you have been awarded a bar to your D.F.C. From what I have heard it is the least that could have happened! My heartiest congratulations and all good wishes for the future.

I am having some trouble with Air Headquarters about Towell's acting rank now that you have been placed in command of the A.T.P., but I hope it will work out all right.

Best wishes,

Yours Sincerely

F.J.C. Vincent

Wing Commander J.L. Beck, D.F.C.,
R.A.F. Station,
Poona.

Congratulations from Air Commodore FJ Vincent CBE DFC.

A typical 'basher'.

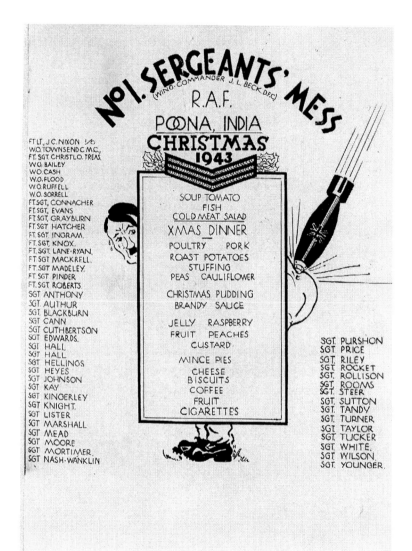

Nº1. SERGEANTS' MESS
(WING-COMMANDER J.L.BECK, DFC)
R.A.F.
POONA, INDIA
CHRISTMAS
1943

FT.LT., J.C. NIXON I/6
W.O. TOWNSEND C M.C.,
FT. SGT. CHRIST LO. TREAS
W.O. BAILEY
W.O. CASH
W.O. FLOOD
W.O. RUFFELL
W.O. SORRELL
FT. SGT. CONNACHER
FT. SGT. EVANS
FT. SGT. GRAYBURN
FT. SGT HATCHER
FT. SGT. INGRAM
FT. SGT. KNOX.
FT. SGT. LANE-RYAN.
FT. SGT. MACKRELL.
FT. SGT. MADELEY.
FT. SGT. PINDER
FT. SGT. ROBERTS
SGT. ANTHONY
SGT. AUTHUR
SGT. BLACKBURN
SGT. CANN
SGT. CUTHBERTSON
SGT. EDWARDS.
SGT. HALL
SGT. HALL
SGT. HELLINGS
SGT. HEYES
SGT. JOHNSON
SGT. KAY
SGT. KINGERLEY
SGT. KNIGHT.
SGT. LISTER
SGT. MARSHALL
SGT. MEAD
SGT. MOORE
SGT. MORTIMER.
SGT. NASH-WANKLIN

SOUP TOMATO
FISH
COLD MEAT SALAD
XMAS DINNER
POULTRY   PORK
ROAST POTATOES
STUFFING
PEAS   CAULIFLOWER

CHRISTMAS PUDDING
BRANDY SAUCE

JELLY   RASPBERRY
FRUIT   PEACHES
CUSTARD

MINCE PIES
CHEESE
BISCUITS
COFFEE
FRUIT
CIGARETTES

SGT. PURSHON
SGT. PRICE
SGT. RILEY
SGT. ROCKET
SGT. ROLLISON
SGT. ROOMS
SGT. STEER
SGT. SUTTON
SGT. TANDY
SGT. TURNER
SGT. TAYLOR
SGT. TUCKER
SGT. WHITE.
SGT. WILSON.
SGT. YOUNGER.

Menu and seating plan for Christmas dinner at RAF Poona, India 1943

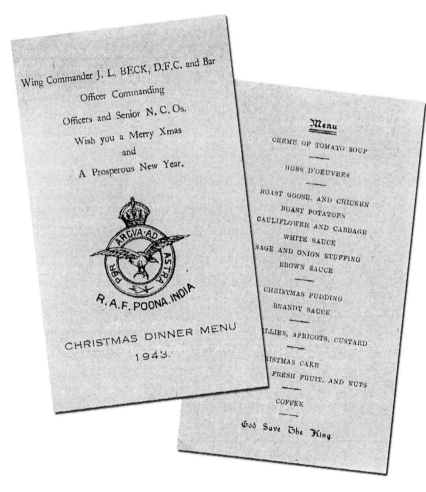

Wing Commander J. L. BECK, D.F.C. and Bar

Officer Commanding

Officers and Senior N. C. Os.

Wish you a Merry Xmas
and
A Prosperous New Year,

PER ARDVA·AD ASTRA

R.A.F. POONA. INDIA

CHRISTMAS DINNER MENU

1943.

Menu

CREME OF TOMATO SOUP

HORS D'OEUVRES

ROAST GOOSE, AND CHICKEN
ROAST POTATOES
CAULIFLOWER AND CABBAGE
WHITE SAUCE
SAGE AND ONION STUFFING
BROWN SAUCE

CHRISTMAS PUDDING
BRANDY SAUCE

JELLIES, APRICOTS, CUSTARD

CHRISTMAS CAKE
FRESH FRUIT, AND NUTS

COFFEE

God Save The King.

Dinner menu served to the Squadron by the officers ~ Poona 1943.

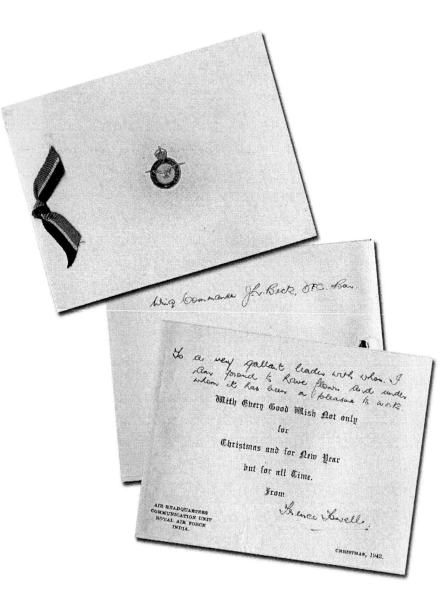

To a very gallant leader with whom I am proud to have flown and under whom it has been a pleasure to work.

With Every Good Wish Not only

for

Christmas and for New Year

but for all Time.

From

Bruce Lovell

AIR HEADQUARTERS
COMMUNICATION UNIT
ROYAL AIR FORCE
INDIA.

CHRISTMAS, 1943.

Wing Commander J.L.Beck, DFC. Bar.

RAF Christmas card given to the Author by a colleague in 1943.

Kirby Green trained with the Author at Montrose. He was murdered by the Germans whilst a prisoner of war in 1944.

Postcard sent from Tel Aviv to Penelope in 1944. The Author on left, Flt Lt Dyer on right.

Penelope (centre) safe in the country after fleeing the bombs of London ~ 1944.

A reply to this telegram may be sent from any branch of Cable and Wireless Limited, the addresses of which will be found in the Telephone Directory, or from any Postal Telegraph Office, using up to three of the following texts, for a charge of 2s. 6d. for a complete message.

CORRESPONDENCE
1. Letter received many thanks
2. Letters received many thanks
3. Telegram received many thanks
4. Parcel received many thanks
5. Parcels received many thanks
6. Letters and parcels received many thanks
7. Letter and telegram received many thanks
8. Telegram and parcels received many thanks
9. Letters sent
10. Parcels sent
11. Letters and parcels sent
12. Many thanks for letter
13. Many thanks for parcel
14. Many thanks for telegram
15. No news of you for some time
16. Writing
17. Urgent
18. Please write or telegraph
19. Please write
20. Please telegraph
21. Please reply worried
22. Airgraph letter received many thanks
23. Letters arriving regularly
24. Have you received letters
25. Your letters not received
26. Please address letters home
27. Have you received telegram
28. No parcel for some time
29. Write same address
30. Parcel sent
31. Writing regularly
32. Your parcels not received
33. Have you received parcel

GREETINGS
26. Greetings
27. Loving greetings
28. Fondest greetings
29. Love
30. Darling
31. All my love
32. All my love dearest
33. All our love
34. Fondest love
35. Fondest love darling
36. Best wishes
37. Greetings from us all
38. Loving greetings from all of us
39. Best wishes from all of us
40. Fondest wishes from all of us

41. Best wishes and good health
42. Kisses
43. Love and kisses
44. Fondest love and kisses
45. Well
46. All well at home
47. Best wishes for Christmas
48. Best wishes for Christmas and New Year
49. Loving wishes for Christmas
50. Loving wishes for Christmas and New Year
51. Loving Christmas thoughts
52. Happy Christmas
53. Happy Christmas and New Year
54. Good luck
55. Keep smiling
56. My thoughts are with you
57. Many happy returns
58. Birthday greetings
59. Loving birthday greetings
60. Happy anniversary
61. You are more than ever in my thoughts at this time
62. Best wishes for a speedy return
63. Good show keep it up
64. Best wishes for New Year
65. May God grant you a year of happiness
66. God bless you and keep you safe
67. My thoughts and prayers are ever with you
152. Love and best wishes for New Year to all at home
153. Best love from daddy
154. God be with you till we meet again
155. God bless you
156. Love to daddy
157. My love and greetings on Mother's Day
158. My love and greetings on Father's Day

HEALTH
68. Family all well
69. All well children evacuated
70. All well children returned home
71. All well and safe
72. Are you all right
73. Are you all right worried about you

74. Please don't worry
75. Hope you are improving
76. Please telegraph that you are well
77. Are you ill
78. Have you been ill
79. Illness is not serious
80. Illness is serious
81. I have left hospital
82. In bad health
83. Health improving
84. Health fully restored
85. Son born
86. Daughter born
87. Am well and fit
88. Delighted to hear you are safe and well
89. So glad to hear that you are better
90. Have not been ill
159. Hope you will soon be better
160. Have not been well
161. Injury is not serious
162. Anxiety anniversary
163. Going into hospital
164. Operation over condition satisfactory
165. Hope children all well
166. Both well
167. Twins born
168. How are all the family
169. Injury is serious
170. I am in hospital

PROMOTION
91. Congratulations on your promotion
92. Very pleased to hear of your promotion
93. Delighted hear about your promotion
94. Have been promoted
95. Have been decorated
96. Have received commission
97. Congratulations on your commission

MONEY
98. Please send me £X
99. Please send me $X
100. Have sent you £X
101. Have sent you $X

102. Can you send me any money
103. Glad if you could send some money
104. Have received money
105. Have you received money
106. Have you sent money
107. Thanks for money received
108. Have not received money
109. Unable to send money
110. Sorry cannot send money
111. Do you need money
112. Have paid £X into your banking account amount to be inserted
113. I do not need money
114. Can you make me daily allotment
171. Have sent money
172. Can you increase the allotment
173. Are you receiving allotment
174. Business very bad grateful financial assistance
175. Expect to be able to send you money next pay day

CONGRATULATIONS
115. Congratulations on anniversary best wishes
116. Congratulations lasting happiness to you both
117. Glad and proud to hear of your decoration everybody thrilled
118. Loving greetings and congratulations
119. Good luck keep it up
120. I wish we were together on this special occasion all my best wishes for a speedy reunion
121. Very pleased to hear you have passed examination
122. Best wishes to all at home
123. Our thoughts are with you
124. Love to all the family

WAR DAMAGE
125. X injured and in hospital
Note—The name to be inserted immediately after the text number.
126. Injured and in hospital
127. Sorry to hear of damage hope all well

128. Sorry to hear of injury and hope not serious
129. Sorry to hear of injury and hope progress favourable
130. Sorry to hear of injury and hope soon be better

MISCELLANEOUS
131. What things do you need most urgently
132. Have done as you asked
133. Rumour not true
134. No
135. Very happy to hear from you desires am fit and well
136. Hearing your voice on the wireless gave me a wonderful thrill
137. Hope to see you soon
138. Hope
139. Your telegram not received
140. Yes
176. xFather } These can be in-
177. xMother } serted in front of
178. xWife } items numbered X
179. xFiancée } hereunder
180. X writing telegraphing frequently
181. X writing weekly
182. X writing regularly, receiving no reply
183. X anxious welfare, no news recently
184. X receiving letters regularly
185. X receiving letters occasionally
186. X well, receiving allotment
187. X recovered operation returning home
188. X is entering hospital
189. Hope to broadcast greetings from BBC listen X
(X—day of week to be added by filer)

BEREAVEMENT
141. Sorry to tell you X died
142. Sorry to hear X died
Note—The name to be inserted immediately after the text number.
143. The Lord bless and sustain you in your loss

HEAD OFFICE OF THE COMPANY: ELECTRA HOUSE, VICTORIA EMBANKMENT, LONDON, W.C.2.
Telegraphic Address: EMPIREGRAM, ESTRAND, LONDON   Telephone: TEMple Bar 1222

CABLE & WIRELESS LIMITED

1HXA430/C 9 29AUG

EFM BECK COTLEIGH
STETCHWORT NEWMARKET

MANY HAPPY RETURNS

YOU ARE MORE THAN EVER IN MY
THOUGHTS AT THIS TIME.

ALL MY LOVE DEAREST

57 61 32 = LEIGHTON

Wartime options for Cable & Wireless messages.

The Author (left) and members of 3rd TAF observing the bombing and IV Corps, 17th Division, Indian Army engaged in a ground attack on Bishenpur against Japanese 33rd Division ~ May 1944.

Members of 3rd Tactical Air Force parachute training ~ 1944.

Wing Commander and Mrs Beck attending a postwar Naval wedding in London.

The Author in UK mess kit ~ 1950s.

Summer holiday camp at Sopley 1954. FCU 3609 ~ now Leeds/Bradford Airport.

3609 FCU Royal (Aux) Air Force ~ Yeadon, Yorkshire 1954. Author fifth from left in front row.

Officers of 3609 FCU present a silver tankard to Wing Commander Beck on his retirement.

Budge with daughters Penelope (right) and Priscilla ("Scilla") ~ 1996.

The Author and wife being entertained by the Governor of Jersey,
Air Vice Marshal Sir John Cheshire ~ Battle of Britain Day 2002.

Wing Commander Beck, as president of the Jersey Kart Club, introduces Air Marshal Sir John Davies
(Lieutenant Governor of Jersey) to competitors at the Bouley Bay Hill Climb ~ Jersey 1973.

A B24 Liberator handed over to the Indian Air Force at the end of
World War Two, now in the Indian Air Force Museum, Delhi.
From right to left Mrs Beck, Lieutenant Colonel Tony Wooley,
Lady J. LeGallais and Wing Commander Beck ~ 1989.

Lieutenant-Colonel Tony Woolley TD ex-Jersey Militia and the Author
attending levee at Government House c1990.

Wing Commander & Mrs Beck ~ 2002.

A well-deserved drink!

By the KING'S Order the name of
Squadron Leader J. L. Beck, D. F. C.,
Royal Air Force,
was published in the London Gazette on
1 January, 1943,
as mentioned in a Despatch for distinguished service.
I am charged to record
His Majesty's high appreciation.

Secretary of State for Air

Mentioned in a Dispatch for Distinguished Service Middle East 1942

DFC & Bar, 1939/45 Star, Africa Star & Clasp, Aircrew Europe Star, Burma Star, Defence Medal, War Medal 1939/45 & Queen Elizabeth II Coronation Medal.

screwdriver had been left in the aileron control on one wing, which jammed its operation.

Although it was nothing to do with our transit pool, I sent condolences to the head of the workforce with suitable wreaths on behalf of the whole RAF station. I was glad that our fire crews had sprayed the flames with foam and saved a few lives.

Another time, when I was coming up to Poona on the train from Bombay, after visiting my Group HQ, the train had just reached the top of the escarpment from the coastal plain when I noticed a commotion ahead and we slowed down. I stopped the train when I realised that a plane had crashed a short distance away, which the driver had seen. I walked over to the scene and found that a Hurricane fighter had dived into softish ground, vertically at high speed. The nose of the aircraft was buried, together with the cannon barrels, which stuck out from the leading edges of the wings. The wings themselves had crumpled and left a bit of the tail sticking out of the ground. Nothing was left of the pilot bar one foot, found close by. I learnt later that the poor fellow was on a training flight and had gone up a valley in this mountainous country in good visibility but the top was covered in cloud. The valley narrowed at the top and he flew up into the cloud, where excessive turbulence must have toppled his artificial horizon instrument. He would be climbing rapidly once in cloud to make sure he got over the top of the Plateau Mountains but without instruments a pilot is absolutely blind in cloud and cannot tell what angle his aircraft is flying at.

I myself had a narrow escape when taking up a Harvard trainer. I had not flown a single-engined plane since 1941. Flying four-engined bombers in comparison is, of course, a different experience. The Harvard had a spring-loaded tail wheel which helped keep the aircraft straight when on the ground in a crosswind (wind air pressure on the tail and fuselage tends to turn aircraft into wind). I had already done several "circuits and bumps" and was rather pleased with myself that I hadn't forgotten how to fly a small trainer when, as I came into land again, I noticed piles of stones distributed at intervals just off the runway which had been dumped there while I was putting the Harvard through its paces. These were close, but I carried on completing my landing. I saw from the windsock that the wind had increased and I was prepared for the possibility of a ground loop. I landed normally and held it straight for a time but the crosswind was so strong that it overcame the tail-wheel spring and the machine went into a ground loop and consequently smack into one of the piles of stones, which were only a short distance away.

The Harvard tipped up gracefully, bending and distorting the propeller. It swayed for a few seconds between tipping right over or staying upright. Fortunately for me it finally settled upright, with me hanging on my straps, looking straight down at the engine and the pile of stones, cursing and swearing at my lack of control, resulting in damage to what had been a perfectly good and sound training aircraft. I was brought to my senses when I noticed a bright flicker of flame leap up from the hot engine. I didn't wait any longer. I banged off my harness, pushed back the sliding cockpit canopy, using all my strength, clambered out and got away in double-quick time, as I expected it to explode in a ball of flame at any second. From a safe distance I sadly watched it go up in flames almost immediately.

So there I was, the experienced Wing Commander Station Commander of RAF Poona, with seven years flying experience, standing there with 'egg all over my face'!

At the subsequent enquiry it was revealed that the pile of stones had been extended far too near the strip when I was doing my "circuits and bumps", which had included me having a look at the surrounding country for half an hour. I was, however, rather shaken, as I had recently seen a Hurricane pilot who had crash-landed, knocked himself unconscious in the process and died in the conflagration which followed. Poor chap didn't stand a chance.

One of my duties as Station Commander was to liaise with the local community, which included the local police, and I had not been there very long before a charming Anglo Indian Chief of Police in that area contacted me and requested my help in disposing of a rogue leopard that was terrorising villagers in the hills south of Poona. He had organised a hunt and in due course I found myself standing near the top of a high pass leading over the ridge into the valley on the other side. It was wonderful country and standing high up we could see a succession of mountain ridges stretching away into the distance, with wooded valleys in between. We could hear the noise as beaters with drums and rattles slowly came up the valley below. There was a short space of open ground from the ridge to the dense cover in the valley below, where the policeman stood, with his heavy-duty shotgun, on the edge of a ravine. I was armed with a service 303 rifle and had no idea what to expect. I thought perhaps that this dangerous animal would charge out of cover and be on to me in seconds, but suddenly out came a herd of black wild pigs, who streaked over the ridge at great speed. Then, just as I was getting fed up waiting, this leopard just strolled out of cover and casually looked around, like a big domestic pussycat. The policeman was quite near and fired. The leopard roared and took three enormous bounds straight onto him and both disappeared into the trees below, but not before I managed to put two rounds into him when he was on the move.

We found the leopard dead under a bush. The policeman had large canine teeth wounds deep in his throat and shoulder. We got him to hospital where his life hung by a thread for three days with blood poisoning (leopards are carrion eaters). He survived and kept the pelt – and I kept the memory of a momentous day.

The village headman congratulated us fervently as that leopard had already carried off and killed several young women engaged in drawing water from the village well.

12/8/43

...Did I tell you I shot a panther or leopard (same thing) in the hills near here. Its part of the training I'm giving the lads to get them hardened and in the open air. We walked miles 15-20 up and down mountains and as an additional thrill they take service rifles to shoot game. I hope to bag a wild boar soon or black buck. If the Panther skin is OK I shall bring it home as a rug for wifie see! Maybe make a coat of it!! "Husband clothes wife" headlines!! I enclose a photo as you said you haven't seen a recent one of me sweet. I hope I don't look too grim or tired and that you still recognise a likeness -- the strain of work is rather taking it out of me these days and that's why I try to take as much sport as possible so that I do not overwork in the office. Isn't he a beauty? The car is my reserve shooting brake which I formally had as a station commanders car – I now have a super "D4 Sota" a big yank saloon in dark Air Force blue.

HQ Southern Army was also based in Poona and as CO of the nearest RAF Airfield I was invited to attend a dinner evening in their mess. All I had was my No.1 Blue standard uniform, so I felt somewhat embarrassed, because all the Army Officers were in full Mess dress. We dined in style, having sherry with the soup after cocktails at reception. The food was of the finest and the cuisine exceptional. Wine flowed and with the mess silver gleaming on the table it was altogether a really fine occasion. I was made very welcome by the General in Command but was amazed to see such extravagance. I had left a country at war since 1939, where luxury like this had disappeared two and a half years ago. Nevertheless I thoroughly enjoyed it; it brought back memories of how things had been pre-war. I realised, of course, that there was no actual war going on in Poona, nor was India under imminent threat. The Japanese army was a long way away, subduing Burma.

Some 70 miles south of Poona, my Group HQ had established a Jungle Training Camp for aircrew, in case they came to grief over Burma and landed in jungle country. My trainees were sent there by crews and were given instructions on how to survive in such an event – what vegetation was nutritious and safe to eat, how to set traps for food and use a survival kit, etc. This kit contained purifying water pills and practical items such as fish hooks, etc. We also carried specially made folding machetes in our flying suits, as well as escape kits containing tiny compasses disguised as buttons or collar studs and silk maps sewn into our battledress.

Crews would be taken out into wild mountainous countryside in closed vehicles and dumped in remote locations without food and they were expected to find their own way back to camp within 2/3, days using only their navigational skills and fending entirely for themselves in wild country abounding in snakes and wild animals.

My own Group HQ in Bombay had asked me to keep an eye on this camp and it had attached to my station two expert botanists and nutritionists. One was the Chief Scientist Mr A.C. Tunstall of the Assam Tea Experimental HQ and Development Station and the other was the well known botanist and author Kingdom-Ward. Both were erudite persons and I thoroughly enjoyed their conversation and company. The first one advised me the best way to deal with an intruder in India at night was to have a large bottle of soda water which in India were shaped like small Indian exercise clubs, on your bedside table. In the event you could hit him over the head and the shock and the loud explosive noise as the bottle shattered would be enough to send him packing. Good advice for sneak thieves maybe but not for Japs.

I visited the Jungle Training Camp only twice. The first visit was rather tragic and the second one involved a rather comical episode. The jungle training camp was located right up in a mountain range in really wild country which was, many years ago, the territory of the Mahratta people who were a warrior tribe of considerable power in India. In the 19th century the British Army had had to subdue their warlike threats to keep the peace of India and in the course of doing so had built a narrow road up to the high country in the Western Ghats to facilitate the movement of cannon. They had used cobble stones in the construction.

4 September 43

...I pray and pray every day that I may get a posting back home as our separation is not easy to bear. Forgive my moan sweetheart but sometimes I feel it so much and my life is not

natural. The bachelors out here are alright as they can go out and join in the normal club life with their girlfriends but the married chap like myself cannot and do not wish to join in on the local social life as we are married to our sweethearts far away and can think of no-one else. The occasional pictures and stag parties in the mess relieve the tension a little fortunately.

I am going on a shoot tomorrow at crack of dawn darling so sorry I won't be with you to get your morning cup of tea!! (cha they call it here). We shall be away by 0630 hrs before sun up. I am taking your advise darling one and not taking any chances by carrying a Sten gun which I have learnt to use. We hope to get some wild boar and pea fowl.

As there was a chance offered to me by an Australian Army Officer instructor to accompany him in his jeep to the camp, I accepted. He said he knew a place high up where we could bag a few peacock for the pot. I had a 12 bore with me and to make up the places in the jeep, Kingdom-Ward came with me. We motored into the mountains from Satara and I remarked that the narrow road up was made of proper cobbling. I was informed then that we were travelling up the very same road which the British Army had constructed in the 19th century. It was remarkably well preserved. Near the top there was a 100 yards of flat scrub covered land leading to a cliff edge with a sheer fall of some 3,000 feet into a jungle covered forest below.

The Aussie parked the jeep and indicated that the strip of land to our right was full of peacock in the scrub so we started walking through with our guns at the ready. Although we banged away at a few shapes flitting through the low covering we got nothing and just out of range ahead we saw these peacocks break cover and launch themselves into space from the edge of the cliff. They were no fools – they knew exactly what they were doing and in my imagination I saw them turn their necks and thumb their noses or beaks at us!

So though disappointed we continued up the road and shortly after a king cobra actually came out of the grass verge and attacked the jeep. Thank goodness all he got was a mouthful of metal and went off rapidly. It was real "cowboy and injun country" – magnificent scenery – pure air and the sun beating down on our Aussie hats (which we all had). We were young, fit and bursting with life. There were two of us in the front and I was in the back with Kingdom-Ward. I and the front passenger had our shot guns at the ready, pointing upwards for safety when suddenly around a bend we came face to face with a totally surprised hyena.

He took one quick look at the jeep, turned and ran for his life. The front passenger peppered his tough backside with spread shot which caused him to tuck in his rear very firmly in at each shot and increase his speed. Then getting into the spirit of the thing our tough but reckless Aussie driver gave chase. Everyone was excited as we got nearer until with a final burst of speed we hit the hyena a glancing blow which deflected the front wheels into a bank at the side of the track. The jeep tipped up and the four occupants sailed over the top in perfect formation and landed ahead sprawled on the ground. Both our shot guns went off as we sailed through the air. We were all shaken but it was a miracle that only one of us had any serious injury. That happened to be Kingdom-Ward who lay on the ground moaning. I cradled his head in the crook of my arm and all he said was "I can't feel anything in my legs, my spine must be broken – tell my daughter I love her" and relapsed into a coma. I was really scared but we got him to hospital and I heard later that he had only cracked a neck-bone and he made a good recovery. At the time of the accident we really thought one of us must have shot him as we went over.

The second time I went I had to stay the night in a dak bungalow at Satara. These were comfortable bungalows on main routes in India where persons of rank and government officials could make an overnight stop. I checked in about 4 p.m. and hearing that there was a club for planters and businessmen up the road where I could perhaps get a sundowner in pleasant club surroundings. I spruced up and set off up the road walking and shortly turned into a driveway leading up to an imposing residence which fitted the description I had been given of the club. I went in and was shown into an elegant drawing room by a magnificently attired bearer and was asked what I would like to satisfy my thirst. I ordered iced whiskey and relaxed on a sofa to enjoy the cool of the evening. I had a couple of stiff ones and began to wonder when a few members would arrive as it was now after six. A white-haired lady then came in and joined me and I surmised, as she was nicely dressed in elegant clothes, that she would be the wife of a member who was waiting for her husband to turn up.

After a bit of light conversation in which I commented on the rather dowdy old curtains, sympathising with her saying how difficult it must be for the club to get new furnishings during wartime. At this she burst out laughing and said "how funny Wing Commander, the club is next door. This is the country residence of the Governor of Bombay Province, Sir David Colville and I am his wife". I was covered with embarrassment but she was charm itself. She pressed me to stay a while so I had another couple of whiskies and thoroughly enjoyed myself. She was interested in what the RAF were doing at Poona and I told her how much my men enjoyed riding the Governor's Bodyguard horses which he had given permission for us to do back at Poona. I left with a glow, slept like a log at the dark bungalow and never forgot the incident of the mix-up.

Next morning I was up bright and early and after breakfast took a stroll down the road to stretch my legs. Shortly I came across an old looking Maharajah's palace. It looked dowdy and much lacking in decor. It was obviously an ancient building and thus interesting. I wandered down to where the elephants were housed and going into a courtyard, through an arched gateway, I saw only one poor old jumbo who was off-white in colour. I was intrigued to discover that his mahout (keeper) was painting him black. On enquiring the reason I was informed that its owner the maharajah was not very well off and as there was to be a procession the following day his elephant was being made to look young again for the occasion! It also struck me for the first time that the Indian arch is just the right shape for an elephant to pass through with that little point at the top for his spine being duplicated in the arch construction.

RAF India Command 14th September 1943

...Sweetheart my depression has left me and I feel 100% better. I think it is largely due to the fact that the low wet, cold monsoon clouds have rolled away and the sun has come out amongst fleecy clouds high up. The sun's brilliance sets off this homely scenery beautifully. My Sweet, this is a lovely place. The bungalow overlooks a large lake which can be seen through an avenue of pine trees. The garden flowers are exquisite and the eucalyptus scent from the Australian blue gum trees pervades the air in a most exhilarating fashion...

...Yesterday I went rowing on the lake in the morning, then down to town shopping with Mrs Norman in their car – she's a great old sport and not a bit crochety despite her advanced age...

...I was dragged out this afternoon by Shotter to see if we could shoot a tiger or panther. We went out 5 miles, walked another 5 but saw nothing but jungle sheep which we are not allowed to shoot.

The country is rolling rather like the South Downs on a much larger scale and the valleys have more scrub in them. It is most strange to know that there are tigers and panthers roaming around in such peaceful surroundings. When we arrived back at the car the chauffeur told us that 20 minutes before – a panther and cub had passed within 20 yards of the car! Did we curse.

As Station Commander I led a busy life. I was responsible for everything on the camp site and aerodrome. After a dance at the Sergeants' mess one night thieves spirited away the safe full of takings by the simple means of cutting a hole in the mud and straw wall of the mess and removing it whole in the dead of night. As I have said before there was no wall or fence around the camp and anyone could just walk in from the surrounding countryside. As Station Commander I was of course ultimately responsible so, any day now I am expecting a large bill to arrive from the Air Ministry!

We had a bit of a discipline problem with aircrew coming into camp late at night somewhat the worse for over indulging in the local hooch, which was a killer. In my wisdom I remembered the WO (discipline) at Uxbridge and I felt that if I could get hold of one of those martinets my problems would be over. I signalled Air Ministry for one to be sent out immediately and he duly arrived. A real toughie, tall and broad. One of the Old School and I was delighted.

Discipline tightened right away for a week then he went into town on Saturday night having been warned of the local hooch. Monday morning he was up before me on a charge of failing in his duties. He had had a night on the local hooch, got blind drunk and stoned out of his mind – jumped onto a bus full of nurses, he careered round town and finally came to grief amongst some trees by the roadside. Sadly I thought to myself what terrible damage bad hooch can do in such a short time. I had no alternative but to send him back. I often thought that he might have been victimised by some so-called friend spiking his drinks. Who knows?

As the base was expanding, local traders honed in on me to get a franchise to provide their services such as the tailor, cobbler or a chap who wanted permission to run a cinema for the troops. They were very genuine people and these services were needed so I made my choices. What I had not expected were the bribes offered which of course I learnt now was quite the norm in business in India. To accept a bribe was anathema to me as a serving officer. A detestable thing to Brits of all ranks and especially for those in authority. So I declined all offers politely and explained why this action was unacceptable

My accommodation was in a private house in Poona. It was three storeys high and my bedroom was on its own at the top. A large metal bed stood in the middle which had seen better days as the netting was rather loose so that I could bounce on it like a trampoline, and it was my habit on retiring to run and leap onto it when I would sink to within a few inches off the floor, then bounce less each time until it came to a luxurious rest. I then learnt that refusing bribes can be detrimental to ones health as one night I did my usual aerial leap onto the bed and half way down I crashed into a hard surface thereby bruising my lower back in the process. Investigation revealed that a large case of whisky in a wooden box had been smuggled in and placed there. Nobody knew how it got there and there were no markings on it. I could not return it without knowing from whence it had come so I shrugged my shoulders and sent it down to our mess bar. It tasted even better than our usual stock. Is there a moral there somewhere?

India Command 1st November 1943

...I too find life rather humdrum sweetheart – married officers without their wives just don't fit in here. I always think its far worse for us than the bachelors who can have quite a good time with the locals who wish to get their pasty faced daughters married off to officers.

I am getting over my Autumnal cold which was rather worse this year as it went down to my chest badly.

I am simply burdened down with work dearest trying to get the station ready for my A.O.C.'s inspection which takes place in the near future, with a full scale peace-time inspection and march past. I feel so tired after work that I normally flop on my bed for 1 hour before dressing for dinner.

I am keeping up my swimming as much as possible and a little golf. I am applying for a move in a month and asking to go to the U.K.!!! or to Bengal again. I feel that if I can't be at a back area station with my wife I don't want the job at all and would rather be up at the front doing a real job.

Exaggerated tales were rife in all RAF units and I expect still are. It was called 'shooting a line'. One which was said to me very seriously in our bar by a very young pilot whom we had worked rather hard, which I thought was a classic. He looked a bit bewildered so I asked him how things were and he said "I'm not quite sure Sir, I've been flying so much lately that I feel a bit lost on the ground"! Another time on the spur of the moment I thought up one of my own. After a particularly grim sortie when my Liberator was being patched up by our ground crew, a visiting army chap said to me "are those holes along the side of your aircraft the result of flak"? "No", I said. "In the RAF we like to go in really low to make sure we hit the target. Those are bayonet holes".

Life was exciting enough in peacetime and far more so in a protracted war. The situation between the "Axis" powers and the allies was changing all the time in this fluid global war. All three services were moving about continually with the ebb and flow of victories and defeats. Life in the RAF was no exception especially as it was the most mobile of our forces, except for Bomber Command's striking force in England pounding mainland Germany from permanent home bases. RAF Squadrons and their support units overseas hardly ever stayed in one place for long. 159 Squadron had already moved three times in the Middle East and soon after I left them at Salboni they were on the move again.

The war situation at the end of 1943 marked a change in the fortunes of the allies. The German advance into Russia had been held up at Stalingrad on the Volga River. The British and American 8th and 1st Army had defeated and driven the German Afrika Corps and the Italian Army out of North Africa and were half way up Italy in mainland Europe. The United States Pacific Fleet had recovered from the devastating Japanese surprise attack on Pearl Harbour which had wiped out much of their fleet and was in the process of capturing Islands nearer to Japan in order to bring their airforce within range of the enemy country. The Japanese navy with its aircraft carriers had been crippled at the Pacific battle of Midway by the United States carrier-borne Pacific fleet and the preparations for the assault on mainland Europe (operation "overlord") was almost ready. The British 14th Army had retreated out of Burma and were building up their forces in the Arakan and Imphal in Manipur State for counter attacking and retaking Burma as well as the Malayan peninsular down to Singapore. South East Asia Command (SEAC) had been formed with Vice Admiral Lord Louis Mountbatten as Supreme Commander. 11th Army Group was created with Lt. General William Slim (Uncle Bill to the troops) put in charge of 14th Army "the forgotten army" (as it was known). Air Chief Marshal Sir Richard Pierse commanded SEAC Air Forces. He was my boss at Bomber Command in 1941 in England. Admiral Sir James Somerville commanded the Eastern Fleet for the Royal Navy. Brigadier (later Major General) Orde Wingate was already operating behind Japanese lines in Burma with his jungle-trained "chindit" force with considerable success.

Staff Appointment 3rd Tactical Air Force

It was at this stage of the war that I had the most interesting posting of my career. I felt I had successfully accomplished the task of creating an efficient aircrew training and staging post at Poona and was thinking about getting into the action again with a Squadron when out of the blue came a posting to the Third Tactical Air Force as "bombing operations adviser" (a Wing Cmdr. staff post) at Imphal.

For the uninitiated an RAF Tactical Air Force is an Air Force allocated solely for use in close support of the Army. In this case the 3ʳᵈ TAF was based with 4 Corps HQ at Imphal. This was the chief town of the isolated Indian border district of Manipur and lay only 38 miles from the Burma border. It was a colourful sprawl of buildings amidst gilded temples and bazaars set about a Maharajah's palace and a section of European bungalows on the outskirts. The whole district was about 200 miles long by about 70 miles across and was about 400 miles east of Calcutta. The mountain ranges ran from the Himalayas in the north down to the Bay of Bengal in the south and were almost an impregnable barrier between India and Burma. Imphal stood in the middle of the a long plain and immediately south was a wide lake some 25 miles long by 14 miles wide called Logtak lake. There were paddy fields in the valley around the lake but the mountains all around were covered in jungle. It was surrounded by high mountains.

30ᵗʰ November '43

...Sweet one – I feel our parting more and more as Christmas grows nearer. I remember so well our Christmas at Wycombe together with our wee babe Penelope and it fairly tears at my heart which is and always has been so full of love for you. I have planned to devote my Christmas to my airmen to lessen the pain and shall fortunately be very busy seeing to their welfare. Concerts, pictures, games tombola, smoking concerts, whist drives and the Christmas dinners at which the officers serve the airmen. I think it will help don't you?

23.12.43

...I shall be extra busy these next few days. On Xmas Day we are having a comic soccer match Officers v Sgts for the

amusement of the men. I've bought a comic long nose for the
occasion. Xmas dinner will also be served by us to the men. In
the evening my station concert party is going to give a show.

At the end of December, 1943 I well remember flying to Imphal
from Calcutta in a communications flight Tiger Moth and having
climbed and scraped over the top of jagged mountain peaks
dropped down into the plain and gracefully landing on the strip. I
taxied to the dispersal area, got out into the crisp air and looked
around. The sun was hot at midday and right overhead casting
little shadow. There was the usual dirty white watch office to
which I reported my arrival but little else was moving in the
shimmering heat except a mangy cat or dog sniffing around.
Clearly this part of the world was peaceful at least for the present.
I reported to 3rd TAF HQ RAF and settled down in my mud and
straw basha (sleeping hut).

Sunday 6th January 1944

...the morning before last I got up at 0660 hrs before day-
break and with two other blokes and a native guide – went
huntin'!! We struck off across country breast high through
some tea gardens 'til we reached the deep valleys or gullies of
bamboo forest. Tell our lovely little daughter Penelope – that
as Daddy's party was making such a noise approaching the
jungle – we disturbed a party of some 5 – 6 wild boar which
rushed off madly down the valley and way before we could
take a shot at them. Its frightfully difficult because one cannot
see more than 15 – 20 yards for the thickness of the bamboo,
creepers and other similar thick vegetation. Next we saw two
large jungle fowl – about the same size as a large pheasant

and the cocks are golden in a similar manner. We let these go as we didn't want to disturb the pig we were after. Well – we stalked and stalked, and waited and waited but nowt did see except a little barking deer which disappeared in no time. However- as our thoughts diminished of succulent roast pork we nevertheless benefited by such an exhilarating healthy walk before breakfast !!

...This letter should be full of good spirit as I am sharing a room with an RAF Clergyman who has just come out from England – Poor chap he doesn't know what he's in for and how hard his work's going to be.

I had a fantastic vibrant life for the next six months from the end of December, 1943 to June, 1944. Lt. General Geoffrey Scoones commanded 4 Corps. He was a tall cadaverous looking man with very shrewd eyes. He looked more like an accountant than a burly army man but he had a good reputation earned in WW1. He was astute and his judgement was sound. My boss was Air Vice Marshal S. F. Vincent who had commanded 11 Group at Uxbridge in the Battle of Britain in 1940 and who had recently been in the retreat from Indonesia and Burma.

RAF India Command Imphal Assam 20.1.44

...I have only been in this present job for two days and find it is different by far from anything I have ever done before. Its an Air Staff appointment on the ops planning side I know very little about it at present but am picking it up by degrees. It means I do quite a lot of flying but not on the good old aircraft I flew on in the Middle East.

This country is a mass of mountains. It's mostly jungle and the climate is as cold as you are experiencing at the moment. What a change !! I am living in a tent with no amenities at all. How I long for a gramophone to keep me company.

Every morning we were briefed on the Army situation by the Corps Commander or by his GSO1 and I soon learnt that the 14th Army was gearing up to fight back, after their defeat in Burma with the object of destroying the Japanese 15th Army which was poised to attack it through Imphal. Our Army was ready as it had retrained its troops in jungle warfare up to and exceeding the Japanese standard so as to be able to beat them at their own game.

4 Corps under Scoones had three Divisions with supporting armour and other Units in the North around Imphal and another Corps of two Divisions in the Arakan some 300 miles south. We in 3rd TAF had adequate squadrons of Hurricane fighters adapted for strafing and bombing for close army support (Hurri-bombers) and Spitfire fighters also. Reconnaissance aircraft and a fleet of Combat Cargo Task Force Dakotas for troop carrying and parachute dropping of armed soldiers or supplies. A formidable task force and the first time when units fighting in the jungle (or surrounded by enemy forces) were completely supplied by air when they were otherwise cut off.

When I arrived the trouble was that Scoones was faced with a dilemma as he didn't know at that time whether the Japs would attack in the south up the coast or in the north through Imphal.

RAF India Command Saturday 22.1.44

...Darling – there is not much I can say about my present job or about the country because of security. I wrote to you

two days ago and I'm sure by now you will know more or less where I am. The country round about is very mountainous and the vegetation is jungle and very thick, at that. We are some 3,000 feet up and the mountains go up to 9,000 feet all around. As we are fairly high above sea level the climate is very healthy. It is bitterly cold at night and I sleep under 5 blankets in my tent. I have a staff appointment which requires a lot of flying about the place in addition to office work. There is absolutely nothing to do here – not even a camp cinema. The food is monotonous but wholesome mostly bully beef. The jungle has to be seen to be believed. Dense matted under-growth and a galaxy of bamboo and other trees rising above the creepers etc. the local natives are mostly Mongolian types, very independent but friendly enough. Nearby are a famous tribe of head hunters !!

Yesterday I met a F/O Scoles (I think his name is) who lives at No 5 Queen Anne's Grove !! he knows Dad as they were in the HG together at the beginning of the war. Fancy us meeting in this far flung outpost !!

I hope to be able to write more frequently now, darling one, about every three days or so as I shall not be so busy as I was at Poona – at least not until things start to happen in this part of the front.

The first thing that happened was that in February, 1944, the Japanese infiltrated through the jungle and attacked the British 15th Corps two Divisions in the south (Arakan) with their 28th Army but this was a feint attacking move to cover up their real intentions. Their little game was soon discovered by Scoones when our reconnaissance planes reported troop and supply movements of great strength going through the jungle leading towards Imphal in the north and still further north to Kohima and Dimapur which was the railhead in Assam, India. The only proper road from Burma into India lay through Imphal.

After careful appreciation of all the intelligence reports particularly the air reports Scoones decided that the main attack was to be in the north through Imphal (thank goodness he was right). We were then alerted as to his needs for close air support. Up to then I had spent my time visiting our front line Squadrons and seeing to their needs. They all looked very young to me but they were well trained and enthusiastic and gave the Army excellent close support when it was needed.

RAF India Command 4th February 1944

...I'm at a place in the Surma valley Assam and everything is a little primitive. Thus , my sweetheart I am penning this chat to you on my knee, using an unfamiliar pen, and small book for a backing. Its all a little difficult but I didn't want you to go without a letter this week. I have been here on a job for 4 days now and expect to be away from my headquarters for as many days again.

It is evening time now, just on six p.m. and the sun has disappeared half an hour ago behind a dense horizon of trees. The sunset is rather magnificent here because I am on top of a ridge some 400 feet above the Surma river valley and away to the north only a short distance rise a magnificent range of mountains some 6-8,000 feet high. As the sun sinks in a red glow it sets alight the tops of the tangled mass of tropical bamboo forest trees which cover the steep valleys on either side of the ridge. Even on top, away to the north there stretches a great belt of trees. There are many tea gardens round about which look very orderly because of the flat topped close cropped tea bushes divided into avenues. Here and there are trim little bungalows belonging to the planters.

Oddly enough it is very cold at nights this time of year. I am sleeping on a string bed (charpay) with three blankets.

Yesterday my darling, on my travels I saw a grand old stork, the old man type who looks like a business man dressed in tail coat and striped trousers. I also saw in the bamboo forest a bunch of baboons (no tails) and two extraordinary birds I simply cannot describe which I have not seen before.

Same address 1ˢᵗ March 1944

...Tonight I have come down from some practice flying (I do <u>NO</u> ops) amongst these hills and having had a bath (tin bath) and my supper I'm feeling tired but happy. And so when I'm feeling like this my thoughts naturally turn to my small world of loved ones whose company I have had so little time in. I pray every night that you and I will come through this beastly separation unscathed and our lives unaltered. I've been away nearly two years now sweetheart and from my heart I can tell you that my feelings of love and affection have increased immeasurably even thru' this long time. It's a very happy thought because I find so many people out here have failing memories of their wives. Some of the poor chaps had only been married a few weeks and naturally they forget so quickly. I feel we are fortunate that we've been thru so much together that the memories are indelible and that is what I find helps me so much in this enforced separation. What do you think darling one?

I hope sweetheart that you have been able to go and stay with the Fielders for a month at least on receipt of my cable. I felt that the Germans are bound to take every opportunity before the invasion of pounding London and also trying out any of their new secret tricks which <u>will</u> cause harm to folks in London from the French coast. When we have that coast then it doesn't matter so much. That is why I wanted you and Penelope to retire to a safe place and watch and wait to see which way the wind blows – I shall be watching it closely here.

Major General Orde Wingate who had his Chindit Special Force operating behind enemy lines in Burma at this period had his operations' rooms a short distance away from 4 Corp's defensive box and we were invited to hear him explain his plan for disrupting vital rail and other communications deep inside Burma. He had a photographic map laid out on the floor of his operations Basha and we all had to take our shoes off as he explained his strategy. He always wore a tropical "Bengal Lancer" type of old fashioned army sun helmet with puggaree cloth and flash. He explained that his forces would fly into Burma to different locations with permanent bases with the object of disrupting the Japs communications and war facilities and to tie down enemy troops.

Towards the end of his talk a double bell suddenly rang out which startled us. It came from an ordinary kitchen clockwork alarm clock on a shelf. Wingate stopped it ringing and then said, "Gentlemen, that is to remind us that valuable time is passing – there is no time to waste" and concluded the meeting.

He launched a long range penetration campaign shortly afterwards and it was going quite well when he was killed when his plane, a twin engine Mitchell B25 crashed into the mountains near

Imphal. I saw this American bomber take off from the Imphal strip because I noticed it took off down wind and took the whole runway to lift off. I did not know who was in it but thought it most unwise due to the proximity of the mountain peaks all around. All they found intact was his sun helmet. He proved to be a real morale booster who helped our army to beat the Jap at his own game of jungle warfare.

April 1st 1944

As you will have gathered from the papers we are very busy and I never have a day off. I usually work day and half way through the night as we are in an "Emergency". We live in a "Box" which is a fortified position into which the numerous units nearby withdraw into at night for safety. There is no danger, darling, but there are always measures to be adopted against sabotage from the Burmans in the pay of the Jap. We've had several air battles recently which have been in our favour. Our greatest personal loss is Gen. Wingate with whom we have been working quite a bit. I met him on some military matter – only a few days ago and had great faith in the man as a leader and a man who knew just how to fight the Japs. Darling your last letter has strengthened me and helped me a lot...

It was in the middle of April just before the monsoon broke in early May that one morning I was attending a meeting with my AOC and his SASO deciding which targets to attack. 4 Corps had told us that our forces were already under attack along the Tiddim Road to the south and that Jap forces were filtrating through on jungle paths from the east and north of our fortified HQ (or box as it was called) but we were still not prepared for what happened next.

During a short interval I was looking out of the window frame (no glass) of our mud basha (hut) when I saw flashes and smoke erupting on and around the airstrip about half a mile away, followed by noisy crumps. It was in fact the really first time we realised that the Japs had arrived and were shelling the aerodrome from the surrounding hills. Here I was – an RAF pilot experiencing what it was like being in the army against a hardened disciplined and ruthless enemy. I have to say that I really enjoyed it.

We were completely cut off from India except by air. The Japanese divisions were all around us with 4 Corps divisions heavily engaged in fluid battles with them. Our orders were to stay put and fight it out to the last man. The army was confident and had great military strength with excellent commanders. The order of no retreat gave a real buzz as we all had no intention of doing otherwise. Morale was high and the RAF were at last achieving air superiority over the Jap air forces.

Lieutenant General Slim's 14th Army, of which 4 Corps took the brunt of the fighting, not only contained and defeated the Japanese 15th Army but started the big push back to re-capture Burma while I was there. The RAF gave them huge support by heavily and effectively weakening Jap strongpoints before the army went in to attack. The RAF Combat Cargo Task Force of Dakotas gave round the clock supplies to army divisions cut off. Occasionally we arranged for some blanket bombing by our Strategic Air Force of heavy bombers (Liberators and Wellingtons). 3rd TAF Hurribombers effectively slowed down the movement of Jap supplies to their army by strafing their lines of communications constantly in daylight. Meanwhile our fighter squadrons (mainly Spitfires) fought hard to gain air superiority over the Japanese Air Force.

Here are a few of my main recollections in that period which stuck in my mind.

➢ It was heaven to be cut off from Group HQ as the paperwork dwindled to practically nothing.

➢ Once I lost valuable sleep all night when I walked about counselling a Flight Lieutenant who was going to blow his brains out after receiving a letter from his wife telling him she had left him for another man. He survived!

➢ I slept with a loaded revolver under my pillow. If the Japs surrounded us and anyone entered my hut it would be a question of shoot first and ask who afterwards!

➢ I was the only one in our HQ who managed to obtain a rather moth-eaten mattress for my charpoy (Indian string bed). For months I slept with another occupant of the bed. My bearer found it one morning. It was a Krait ~ a deadly venomous snake. He was under the mattress in some loose stuffing. He apparently appreciated my warmth at night.

8th April 1944

...Re the London raids and your staying at Hambledon. My opinion darling is this. The Hun will raid London in retaliation of our devastating attacks on his cities – until the invasion starts. But a week or so before the Invasion he will be busy pounding the Invasion ports. After the Invasion has started I think he will have to concentrate on our supply ports and will have little time to waste on throwing bombs away on London. So my darling I would like you to be at Hambledon until you see that the Hun is starting to bomb the South Coast

ports which will be the invasion preliminary. This will lessen the risk of London raids and will be the time to move back OK? It is so hard to lay down any hard and fast time but I think you will be able to judge quite accurately at home as to when you will be able to go back – If any peculiar types of bombs arrive on London which are <u>not</u> dropped by A/C then I think it would be wise to move out until you can see just what the effect of them is. I simply could not bear anything to happen to you or Penelope as you well know...

...We are having a tough fight on our front but have no doubt at all that the Jap will be cleaned up. He is very near now but we are all prepared to move to the attack i.e. The army, the RAF is adequately prepared to beat off any infiltration attacks and we all go around armed to the teeth. I have 1. Rifle, 2. Sten gun, 3. Revolver, 4. Knife! So will be quite safe – Don't worry at all.

In the early part of my posting we had Japanese air attacks and the warning at Imphal was three sharp cracks from a Bofors low flying anti-aircraft gun repeated twice. One never forgets air raid warnings. In England it was the wailing siren continually being turned on and off with the all clear as a continuous wail.

As soon as 4 Corps, under Lieutenant General Scoones, realised that the main thrust of the Jap 15th Army was to be against Imphal and Kohima in the north, the Supreme Commander Mountbatten and Lieutenant General Slim, with the help of the British and American CCT Force Dakota Fleet, transferred the 4th and 7th Indian division by air from the Arakan to Imphal. I went down to the airstrip to watch them fly in. It was a wonderful sight to see these two army divisions unload with all their military equipment and hundreds of mules. Thank God for air power for the army as it ensured total victory by bringing reinforcements to 4 Corps in this manner. The Japs did not have this capability and their supply line was badly stretched.

For experience I went out twice with the Army to witness the battles with the Japs. The first occasion was a divisional attack to wipe out a Jap stronghold in a well developed deep bunker system, fortified with wire and mines. It was vital to remove it as it commanded a position overlooking the only road back to India north of Imphal.

Long before dawn on a very dark night I went up to the assembly area. The troops were already moving out up to the start line along narrow paths marked by white tapes indicating the route that had been cleared of mines and booby traps. Everything was done in a hushed silence as it was to be a dawn attack. Although silence was the order of the day I could hear the clink of harness metal on webbing as men went by and the surprise of all was that for 50 yards ahead I could hear the soldier's teeth chattering both with cold and fear. I felt sure mine would have done the same if I had been them.

When they had gone I took up my position with an Artillery Forward Observation Post (FOP). The army spotters immediately dug slit trenches. I had no entrenching tool so I selected the thinnest and smallest man's slit trench to jump on top of if we were shelled. As soon as it was light enough the battle began. The enemy bunker was about ¾ mile away – well camouflaged but just visible through field glasses. It was halfway up the side of a large valley a little below us. The main road was to our left in the middle of the valley. Suddenly our artillery opened up with a deafening noise and the attack went in from both sides of the valley with the rattle of machine guns, mortars and small arms fire. Flashes and crashes all over with artillery guns and mortar fire and spurts of earth erupting all over the bunker. At the same time I heard in the distance the battle cries of the various Indian and Gurkha battle formations as they moved up towards the bunker. They were held up for a time and then a squadron of our heavy tanks moved up from the floor of the valley, leisurely took up their positions, and then blazed away with solid shot to penetrate into the bunker. In a couple of hours the position was taken after fierce resistance and mopping up operations then began.

To me it was a revelation to witness this operation. The bravery and dedication of the soldiers left me 'spellbound' with admiration to think that this was only one of many battles before and after which went on all the time around Imphal. During the siege of Imphal our fighter squadrons flew out at night over the mountains into airfields in Assam returning next day at dawn. They were on call all the time if the army wanted them to bomb and strafe enemy positions. They moved out at night because the Japs were adept at night attacks on aerodromes. RAF Regiments guarded the strips during the "Siege of Imphal".

My next and final trip with the army came about because I wanted to see how our RAF Forward Radio Control Units attached to army formations, succeeded so well in assisting army units by softening up the Jap bunker fortifications just before an attack went in by calling up our Hurri-bomber squadrons whenever they were needed and directing them onto their targets.

I was attached to 63 Brigade commanded by Brigadier Guy Burton (Indian army 17th division) who was under orders to move and clear the hills of units of the Jap 33 division SW of Imphal. The Brigade assembled in a small hamlet which was concealed in a village amongst thick bamboo clumps a half mile at right angles to the east of the main road south of Imphal towards Bishenpur. The connecting road was raised above paddy fields and was in clear view of Jap forces about 4-500 yards away down the main road south. The Brigade of about 3000 soldiers moved silently into the hamlet only at night as it was in front of Imphal's front line and in full view of the enemy and the Japs had no idea we were there. We lay in ditches talking in whispers and no movement was allowed. We had a vast lot of mules which had to be kept quiet. These mules carried all our supplies of food, ammunition and military equipment. No fires or smoking were permitted or anything else which might give our position away. On 18th May, the whole brigade moved out on a dark night into the hills to the west after crossing the main road. All I know was that we were going into battle with the aim of destroying the Jap 33 division before it could reach corps HQ Box at Imphal. I had an RAF Sergeant Radio operator and two mules carrying our radio sets. I followed in the darkness with the leading company for most of the night stumbling about here and there on uneven ground pretty well all the time in the dark.

As dawn broke the brigade found itself out of its intended position exposed in quite open country. I guessed something was wrong as the Brigadier was soundly berating an unfortunate young signals Lieutenant who was supposed to have known the route. As it was getting light Burton ordered the Brigade to take cover in a nullah (ravine) where the mules could be concealed. In no time at all the troops were in position and well dug in. Each person dug slit trenches and when I finally got a spare entrenching tool I thrashed about only to find rock wherever I struck. I was getting desperate as the Japs had spotted us and started shelling. This was a new experience for me. My media was in the air where I could perform brilliantly (so I thought) but here on the ground I was less than adequate. I could hear distant "cracks" followed a few seconds later with an immense "whoosh" and an enormous "bang" with a flash, smoke and bits flying all over the place with blast pressure waves. The larger shells were different. I just heard the whoosh followed by the enormous bangs with greater disruption. A friendly 1st West Yorkshire officer allowed me to share his slit trench and peering out of it I was amazed to see the Brigadier just strolling about as if nothing was happening giving orders.

In no time at all, he had dispatched two companies of Ghurkhas to seize our original target which was the village of Kha Aimol which they took quite easily as the occupying Japs were taken by surprise and fled up to their nearby bunker strong point. We moved into the village and dug in. I was well dug in under the village meeting house of bamboo and matting construction, with a company of Ghurkhas and settled down for the night.

That night it was very dark and moonless. Our orders were to keep absolutely silent so as not to give away our fortified perimeter position and sure enough as was their practice, the Japs came around searching for us. We could hear the occasional clink or rattle of equipment and now and then a high pitched Japanese voice would ring out in English. "Tommee, Tommee – I see you – ha ha, ha ha we come kill you – ha ha". It was unbelievably weird and frightening and for the second time in the war my hackles stood up on the back of my neck. No doubt the troops were used to this tactic of the enemy who used to try to draw our fire to find out if they could break through our perimeter for hand to hand close quarter fighting. Nobody made a sound and after a time we could just hear them going away back to their bunker. I was so glad to be amongst the Ghurkhas as they seemed to actually enjoy fighting. When they were ordered into battle they would smile whilst sharpening their kukris and oiling their tommy guns.

Next day it was hot and sunny and I found our troops washing their socks and clothes in a mountain stream in full view of the enemy around 200 yards away. When I pointed this out they said there was little danger as the Japs had been up all night and would not fire as it would destroy their sleeping in daytime if our artillery opened up on them. Fair enough, I thought, they know what they are doing. That afternoon the Brigadier sent the brigade to capture a hilltop nearby which was heavily fortified with their usual bunker system. I arranged for a squadron of Hurri-bombers to be called up to bomb the position to soften it up, after which the mortars opened up and finally the infantry went in and after bitter hand to hand fighting completely destroyed the enemy. There was one Jap survivor whom I saw, he looked half starved and disease ridden. The brigade captured two artillery 75 mm mountain guns and the pay chest of currency notes over-printed by the Japanese Government.

25th May 1944

...I have been on a special job with the Army for the past 7 days from the 18th to 25th and have been living with forward troops at a brigade H.Q. on an advance. This show has proved most exciting – we moved about in this hilly country as an armed body quite capable of taking care of ourselves but always open to attack. We had nothing but the clothes we stood up in and 3 days hard scale rations but a job of work to be done. I had some RAF radio equipment with me as an experiment and that's why I was with the forward brigade. Everything had to be carried on mules or on our own backs

and it was hard work indeed "sweetheart" We have been continually shelled, shot at but able to carry out a successful operation in the face of many setbacks. For the first time I have really seen large numbers of dead Japs. At the same time I have been able to appreciate the hard conditions under which the Army out here has to fight in this hilly country. When it rains its dreadful – everything is knee deep in mud and the wounded have a dreadful time getting away. I was with a Gurkha regiment and I will say they are the worlds finest little fighters. Tell you all about it when I get home oh dear what a long time to wait...

Having been satisfied that the RAF Forward Radio Control Unit worked well and that the equipment was robust enough to be carried about on mules I left on the fifth day, having thanked Brigadier Guy Burton for allowing me this experience. I walked down the hills to the main road feeling very vulnerable. The enemy were milling around all over the place and were often where you'd least expected them. I had my Smith and Wesson .38 revolver with a sten gun (automatic gun) for close quarters and my aircrew machete. I kept my eyes skinned for Japs and was prepared to sell my life dearly if I was attacked.

I got back to the main road and found a small group of our wounded waiting for transport back to our lines at Imphal. The road was straight for about a mile before disappearing around a small hillock. Half way along a truck had been hit and set on fire by a shell from guns ranging in from the hills and had toppled over alongside the road. Our position was invisible to the Japs as we were behind large bamboo clumps. Several ambulances and other vehicles had built up along the road behind us and no one ventured further whilst the road was under attack in clear weather.

A short while later our gunners put down a smoke screen masking the road. I got into one ambulance driven by an American volunteer and on the word "go" 4 or 5 trucks together went hell for leather down the road. We passed the stricken truck at speed and from my front seat I saw a really fierce battle going on in the paddy fields and bamboo clumps not half a mile away. The Japs and our troops were milling around fighting it out to the death with infantry and tanks. In this type of fluid warfare there is no front line just Brigades, Battalions, companies, and platoons engaged in life and death struggle.

We stopped once to pick up a wounded sepoy (Indian soldier) who had been shot in the foot and sped on until we rounded the hillock out of sight and to our amazement right there in front of us was an immaculately dressed Army Red Cap directing traffic as if he were in Piccadilly Circus on point duty.

During the time I was away there had been a decisive battle at the south end of Imphal town when the Jap 33rd Division's main force had been utterly destroyed. The 31st and 15th Jap Division fared no better at Kohima except that they had blocked the supply route north from Imphal to India, thereby denying 4 Corps any supplies for 86 days. This had been foreseen by 4 Corps HQ who had arranged for the RAF Dakota Force to fly in adequate supplies.

When I got back there was terrible evidence of the Jap final assault. All along the ditches along the road and in front of our defences were hundreds of Japanese infantry who had been killed. Their faces were black as they had been there for two days and their corpses were thick with flies. Destruction was everywhere. Dead and blown up military mules were everywhere with their legs sticking up. It was a dreadful sight and the Army were using bulldozers to bury the corpses. Everyone had their mouths and noses covered with scarves soaked in some yellow antiseptic gauze.

The monsoon broke and turned the ground into mud making it so much harder for the troops as there were still loads of pockets of the enemy out in the hills all around. My admiration for the Army Divisional and Brigade Commanders soared even higher. The Gurkhas, Indian and British infantry were magnificent.

I must relate one event which was rather bizarre – when I was first at Imphal before AVM Vincent arrived. Our Air Officer Commanding was an eccentric Air Commodore whom we called Rolly Polly (our nickname). He was an old timer engineer officer in the RAF and had a rough time retreating with the army out of Burma in 1943. He was fun in an off beat sort of way and he kept a large cat which used to follow him about.

When we had a meeting every morning to decide on the targets for the day the cat (which was known as "Kat") used to lie on the floor in the sun and if there was a diversion of opinion he would ask the cat to give its decision before making up his mind. All this we thought to be odd but fun and helped to keep up morale after the retreat. After all, at that period, due to tension there were quite a lot of oddities around. I remember one airman who simply couldn't use normal prose in writing letters to his wife. He had to rhyme every two sentences as I discovered when censuring his mail. Another chap would loose a week's sleep and go nearly berserk if he discovered he had unwittingly put on odd socks. Another example was when a rear-gunner reported sick as he thought he was going mad – he told the M.O. that when he had his sandwiches on a long flight – he would centre his turret – open the doors at his back and place his pile of grub on the floor behind within easy reach. For a number of sorties he said he saw his sandwiches walk away down the fuselage on their own! He thought he was suffering from hallucinations. The M.O. reported this and on investigation we found that a rat had got into his aircraft and of course it couldn't be seen in the dark at night. There were many examples but in the life we led we accepted these idiosyncrasies as normal. At one time Air Ministry sent out psychiatrists to deal with these oddities but they were sent back because we all thought they were peculiar.

During the early part of the siege of Imphal when we were surrounded by the Japs – Lord Mountbatten, the supreme Commander of SEAC visited 4 Corps HQ to give us an update on the situation and a pep talk to all the Squadron pilots. We were all assembled in an informal way in a largish hut which was crammed and pilots were leaning through the windows as the room was not large enough for all of them. There was one old settee in the middle of the room and the sole occupant was the AOC's Kat which had a large bandage wrapped around its body which had somehow inadvertently got in the way of a .22 bullet but was recovering.

Mountbatten the C in C came in and seeing the pilots looking through the open windows instantly, and in no uncertain manner, ordered the space cleared on the settee. For a second or two there was a hushed silence until someone gingerly removed the AOC's cat.

That was enough for Mountbatten, the next day our Air Commodore was released, tour expired and sent back to England. I was detailed to fly him back to Calcutta and I picked him up at an airstrip due west of Imphal. The strip was on the ridge of high ground at around 5000 feet on a tea plantation and as it was midday I knew it would take the whole length to get off as there was little wind. I taxied to the very end of the runway and opened up the throttle of the Avro Anson communications aircraft with quite a load of passengers in the back. It didn't take up speed all that quickly and I only just got airborne right at the end of the runway and even then I couldn't gain any reasonable height so much so that I just clipped the top of some trees as I climbed gradually. It was touch and go and my heart was in my mouth but gradually I gained enough height. I wondered why until I looked around into the body of the plane. No wonder it seemed unduly heavy. The Air Commodore had opened a large wooden crate in the middle and his bearer was handing out large gin and tonics to all – in fact, they were having a hilarious party and couldn't have cared less about anything. When I landed at Dum Dum (Calcutta) airfield I taxied to a concrete dispersal and swung around into wind and a large part of the tail fell off. On inspection I found the part riddle with termites. A lucky escape!

June 10th 1944

...I cannot tell you my exact movements darling but left Imphal for Delhi on the 1st June – I was held up in Calcutta for a time through transport problems but eventually finished business there on June 5th. As I have a few days to spare I thought I'd pop up to Kashmir state and take a look around while I had the chance and as it is North of Delhi. So off I popped – If I'd known it was so difficult to get here I wouldn't have come – it took me 2 ½ days travel by rail, car and the last 5 miles by mountain pony !! I was going to Scrminager which is the capital of this state but decided on Gulmorge as it is about 5,000 feet higher (9000 feet up !!!) and much cooler

and the Sturgess family are here which is good company for me.

I am staying at a "Miss Christie's Hotel" which is a very prudish quiet family place but suits me as I want rest most of all. I only expect a few days here darling before I proceed to the course – I have been shopping and you will receive in due course some very lovely gifts from me which I wish so much to give you darling Budge because I love you so much and wish you were here.

A day or two after I returned to Imphal the new AOC flew in with his own Hurricane fighter. He was Air Vice Marshal S. F. Vincent who early in the war at Northolt commanded the Polish Fighter Squadrons during the Battle of Britain. Mountbatten chose well, although approachable he was strict and his enthusiasm and experience as a fighter pilot himself in the UK and Malaya was a fine example for our pilots. Morale was sky high particularly as the RAF and US Air Force had finally got air superiority over the Jap Air Force.

Middle East – Junior Staff College

Thus ended a very interesting period of my service life with experience in close army co-operation with 4 Corps at Imphal in the 3rd Tactical Air Force. In early June, 1944, I was once again on the move – this time a posting to the Army Air Force Staff College at Haifa in Palestine. I made the journey as a passenger in much comfort as it was in a Short Sunderland flying boat. It took off from Bombay and landed on the Dead Sea in Palestine (now Israel). This sea is much more solid than normal ocean water owing to the concentration of salts due to it having no outlet and with the heat in that part of the world, a high evaporation rate. The pilot came in very carefully at his slowest speed and even so it hit the water as if it were made of concrete (or so it seemed to me).

M.E. Staff College 23 June 1944

…I have some sad news of Kirby Green. I have just heard from fellows here that he and Mike Casey (another Montrose chap) were shot whilst escaping from a German prison camp. Poor Maria – I feel so sorry for her after what she's been through. I was speaking to S/Ldr Hillier only the other day in Calcutta and he was telling me all about his wife and Maria and what they were doing etc. It'll be a terrible blow to her.

Middle East Staff College 4th July 44

…The house has a small garden all round and the flowers in it are simply gorgeous. The outside walls and porticoes are mainly covered with vivid Bougainvillaea, Wisteria, and Honeysuckle. One poritco has a grape vine entwined round its supports. You can imagine my darling what a delightful scent is wafted round the house all day long.

The remainder of the garden has roses, masses of a type of carnation, geranium, flox, petunias and a variety of lovely sub tropical trees.

We have a house cat. Not beautiful like Boo-Boo. But nevertheless companionable. There is also a resident chameleon he is about a foot long from head to tail, and changes colour perfectly on different backgrounds. Penelope would love to have it as a pet I'm sure. Two happy little Bullfinches live in the Bougainvillaea outside my window, they have crests on their heads.

My room is on the first (top)floor. It is completely distempered in white and has a light green tile floor. It is about ten foot square and contains my bed a big work table, hanging cupboard, dressing table and lastly a chair. There are no windows but opposite the door, double French-windows lead onto a small balcony.

The syllabus is comprehensive. We learn all about the organisation of the Air Force. How to write all types of correspondence, reports, appreciations, essays precis etc. We also have to give lectures, Hubb's great horror ! and hold discussions of all kinds. An important part, of course is planning operations and otherwise running the Air Force in each of its different sections. It is of course tutorial but after we leave here we may have to put any part of what we've learnt into real action. I find it very interesting but by no means easy and we are worked hard. Your encouragement, Budge darling, has helped me tremendously and I hope, God willing, I shall pass OK.

Middle East Staff College. M.E.Forces 8th July 1944

...The wretched buzz-bombs are still hitting London I see by the papers. Their presence causes me no mean anxiety Budge. Are you safe even at Hambledon? I pray and hope the Allied Expeditionary Force will soon have captured so much of France that their bases will be out of reach for launching. I am anxious for our families too.

Please darling, tell me more about conditions at home. We get so little about these things and with it helps me to get a better picture of your daily life. How are you off for clothes? Are we saving much and in what way? Is it time to have Penelope's teeth examined? ...

Middle East Staff College 1944 Saturday 5ᵗʰ August

...Thank you my sweet for writing to Maria about poor old Kirby. I feel very cut up about the whole affair and it has made me more bloody-minded about the Germans...After the shooting affair of Royal Air Force officers I cannot express my hatred of the Germans in words, not hatred perhaps but cold fury. It might so easily have been me instead of Kirby. What a lot of sorrow those thugs have brought into the world. Here in Palestine one sees the suffering on people's faces and many of them have only recently come out of occupied Europe...I think about you so much Budge dearest and so often nowadays I feel sad and terribly lonely. Without you and Penelope life is drab and without meaning.

At the College we were housed 4 officers to each small detached house near the College with patios in front above which grapes were grown on pergolas. In season when I was there it was wonderful to stroll outside and pick ripe bunches of grapes. Porcupines were quite a common sight in the gardens as well as many lizards which darted off over walls even with people in the rooms.

The town squares were full of Jewish refugees from Europe, Germany and Russia in particular (mostly intelligentsia, doctors, scientists and highly qualified musicians). It was quite a common sight to see these mainly bearded men sitting about playing exquisite music for money as they had no other way of making a living. A hotel on Mount Carmel had been taken over for the staff college. It was situated in a high class residential area, well shaded with trees and having lovely open squares for people to prome-nade or sit out in alfresco cafés where musicians played.

The course lasted three months and each intake, consisting of some 30 – 40 officers who were split up into syndicates (small groups), representing different parts of the armed services. In one syndicate there may be a Fighter and Bomber pilot with an aero engineer or RAF Regiment (Defence or Airfields) Officer together with an Army, Infantry, Artillery, Sappers, and Tank Officers etc. All with recent operational experience.

To start with most of the time was taken up with lectures in which syndicates learnt about the various weapons in use, how they were operated and the tactics used in actual recent battles in the Middle East and India/Burma. Lectures also on how an Army and Air Forces moves about and how it is supplied and fed.

It was interesting also to hear how the Top Commanders planned their operations and how they allocated enough forces to defeat an enemy force opposing them and the vital information about the enemy from the combined forces intelligence organisa-tion. We were privileged to have special lectures from Field Marshal B. Montgomery of Alemein fame, Air Marshal Sir John Slessor on bombers and Air Vice Marshal Sir Keith Park, one of the Air Commanders in the 1940 Battle of Britain fighter operations. The last named AVM was a tall good looking Fighter 'Ace' who I think must have fancied himself as a dandy. He was dressed in full No 1 uniform made from special material and very smart with all his decorations of medal ribbon prominently displayed on his immaculate tunic. During his talk it got hot in the lecture room so he stopped and took off his uniform tunic, folded it up and carefully placed it on a chair. Then he turned around facing us and I couldn't believe it. His shirt with medal ribbons was an exact copy of the tunic he had just taken off – in every detail. It tickled me so much that I couldn't help smiling at such blatant vanity. I imagined that at night his pyjamas might also have the same regalia on them.

The middle part of the course was much enlivened by demonstrations, two of which were thrilling experiences. The first one took place in the scrub covered rugged interior in the hills to the north east of Haifa and consisted of a demonstration of an attack by an armoured division. For part of the manoeuvres I rode in a heavy tank over rough ground. Rumbling along on very uneven ground in a tank is no picnic as the occupants are tossed about in the confined inside space where there is ample opportunity for bruising on gun equipment, shell storage racks, radio sets and the like while racing along. Sitting up in the commander's place with the top open I could see the squadron of tanks on either side with infantry keeping up as best they could. The tank guns were banging away furiously and I could see the strikes as the shells burst in the distance. When the top was closed the inside air was full of the smell of cordite and it was extremely hot and uncomfortable.

In the middle of the mock battle I saw to my left about half a mile away two squadrons of self-propelled guns suddenly race up a track overlooking the valley. They stopped on a high spot and sent salvo after salvo off in double quick time and in 5 minutes they were gone again. The noise was terrific and the sudden silence afterwards was deafening in contrast. These and the tanks demonstrated awesome fire power to me and I certainly would not have liked to have been on the receiving end of that lot.

Another day we were taken out into the Mediterranean in a captured Italian navy destroyer. By God, it was fast! It was nearly all engines, quite large but it could do 50 knots flat out. I remember the single light gun near the bows and being able to push the protection shield in with my thumb to make a dent. I thought it would be thick armour plating and I am quite sure it would not even stop a rifle bullet. The larger guns were at the rear so as to be more effective in defence when beating a hasty retreat! We were there for an RAF exercise in which a Wellington Squadron from Egypt had the task of locating us by airborne radar. It was successful as they came swooping down on us dropping bags of flour instead of bombs needless to say. No wonder the 'Ities' can make super speedboats with excellent engines – just look at their Ferrari racing cars!

The staff college course was thorough though concentrated into three months. There was a lot to learn and absorb. Each member of the course had to give a talk to the course on some experience and when my turn came along; I chose to tell the course about the leopard hunt in India. This went down well despite the fact that I tended to overstate the obvious on several occasions quite unnecessarily which caused a certain amount of merriment. For example, when describing the job of the beaters who were driving the game and the leopard up the valley with shouts and rattles I said "and as the beaters came nearer and nearer the sound they were making got louder and louder" (well of course it would, silly ass). The audience could see that the speaker was above nervous and of course time was getting on in the hot sticky afternoon and it was enough to send a ripple through the hall. These things happen when you do this sort of thing for the first time. C'est la vie!

We also learnt how field hospitals were organised and the same night the team of Indian Army Doctors invited us over for dinner at their tented camp not far away along the coast. They gave us a great welcome at the entrance to their dining marquee and they were truly impressive in their colourful mess kit. The Sikhs in their bright turbans and beards were magnificent as most of them were tall. About forty of us sat down to dinner with the tables beautifully laid out with white table clothes with regimental silver gleaming under red shaded table lamps. We had about six courses of expertly cooked Indian fare, curry of course with all its bits and bobs all perfectly cooked and served. A most enjoyable evening and when we came out into the starlit night I complimented the Commanding Officer on the meal and told him that we didn't see any kitchen tents when we arrived. He just pointed to a row of a few brick or mud ovens on the ground a short distance away containing the remains of glowing embers of wood and said the whole meal had been cooked on those small Indian cooking contraptions – amazing!

While at the Staff College a group of us were invited to visit a "kibbutz". These were Jewish collective agricultural settlements in Palestine administered communally by members where children were reared collectively. These settlements were fairly new at that time and as they were away from the coast and out in the interior they had been attacked by local Arabs who saw this heavy influx of persecuted Jews from Europe as interlopers in their land although I believe Arab landowners had sold the land to Jewish farmers who were certainly making better use of the soil by growing varied crops and not just for grazing goat herds. For over half a century the fight still goes on in Israel as the Palestinians feel they were dispossessed of their land to this day.

These settlements in my time were defended by the settlers themselves and had concrete watch towers to give the alarm if an attack took place. Each settlement had its own defence force ready to retaliate if Arab Terrorists started taking pot shots at the Jewish farm workers in the fields. The Settlers were well housed and fed. Each taking turns to prepare food and cook and clean the tables while others worked in the fields. They received no wages but had their keep and a little pocket money. They had to get permission to go into town (Tel-Aviv). The most suitable people looked after the children and the parents had playtime with their children after returning from the fields at night. The food was wholesome and in abundance. They were a rural community of young men and women who were strong and fit and bronzed in the sun. A marked contrast to the Jewry one met in England who were mainly in the luxury businesses.

Palestine is a lovely country steeped in history from biblical times (Old Testament and New Testament at the time of the Roman occupation) followed by the rise and conquest by the Arabs under Saladin who drove the Crusaders out of the country. Then it was conquered by the Turks and became part of the Ottoman Empire. Finally Great Britain who had chased the Turks out at the end of WW1 was given the administration of it as a Protectorate by the League of Nations. It was also to become "a home for the Jews" but not a State.

Even while I was operating from Palestine in 1942 and whilst attending Staff College in 1944 there were two terrorist groups of Jews working "underground" to force Britain out of that role so that they could get the League of Nations to agree to the creation of a Jewish State. (Presumably because way back in biblical times they occupied that land after Moses had led the Israelites out of Egypt according to their version of history).

These terrorist groups were already stealing arms and equipment from the three services and letting off bombs in cinemas and other public places while I was there. One of our liberators returning from a long range mission ran out of fuel and crashed in the Negev. By the time we got there the stern gang or similar terrorist gang had stripped the aircraft of all its machine guns and ammunition (the aircraft had attempted to land on what looked like flat sand but was in fact sand dunes and it broke up killing the whole crew of eight).

During weekends I visited Nazareth (which was a small village on rather a bare rocky hillside). Bethlehem and Jerusalem. On the way into Jerusalem our bus collided with another travelling in the opposite direction. It scraped along one side and shattered the elbows of several passengers who had unfortunately left them outside. There were screams and panic and those poor passengers, mostly local men and women and two American GIs were in a real bloody mess. I was fortunate to have been on the other side. The bus pulled into a wayside cafe forecourt and it was not long before ambulances arrived to take the victims to hospital. A nasty experience which I never want to see repeated. These things happen so quickly when least expected.

In Jerusalem I walked the Via Dolorosa (the street that Christ walked carrying his cross up to Calvary where he was crucified). The church of the Holy Sepulchre is built over this site and inside I saw a stump of wood in the exposed bare rock which was purported to be the remains of the actual cross on which Christ had died. All around the inside of the Church were small chapels.

Each one representing the different sects of the Christian Faith (R.C., Greek orthodox, etc).

It was a moving experience as I prayed earnestly in there for the preservation and safety of my family back in England, as I did in all these places to whichever part of the world I was posted. On leaving I noticed that the entrance was guarded by a Moslem and learnt that it was because the Christian churches inside couldn't agree on who was to have the key and be in charge of the entrance. Afterwards on reflection I wondered what chances our Christian churches had of uniting. Even today, over half a century later, unification is still a far off dream.

At the end of the course, by way of a final exam, each syndicate was given a military operation to plan. This was a daunting task but it was logical as it combined all the subjects we had learnt about the role of each armed service.

First we were given an outline of the task required of us which involved a sea and airborne attack on a certain piece of enemy held territory, to make a successful landing and to consolidate a firm bridgehead ready for further operations.

This meant writing a full military appreciation of the situation as we saw it and to show in broad outline how we would go about achieving the object and the destruction of the enemy. This involved examining the courses open to ourselves as well as the enemy and to decide and recommend the best course to be taken.

Our job as the RAF representatives was to provide an outline plan of the type and number of aircraft required to deal with enemy Air Forces until an airfield could be captured and made safe to operate from, followed by the rapid build up of reinforcements of Army Units to be flown in by troop carrying planes. Provision had to be made for continuous supplies of military equipment to be flown in to sustain the operation and for casualties to be flown out. The weather and terrain had also to be examined closely as bad weather and difficult terrain could greatly hamper operations for success or failure.

The whole document took about a week to prepare and have typed out into a dossier with everyone in our syndicate working flat out on their particular subjects and we handed it in with much relief with about five minutes to spare.

During the few days after hearing I had passed the course we tasted fleshpots of the town which were mostly night-clubs packed with people in small rooms full of cigarette smoke with a hubbub of noise in a stuffy atmosphere. The blackout over windows made it worse and the only relief was in getting somewhat pie-eyed and leaving with your friends and getting back safely in case terrorists were about.

I had the opportunity to spend a few days in Beirut, Lebanon, further north up the coast. I hitched a ride in the back of an empty army truck which was a real bone-shaking experience. There had been civil war there a short time before and the Army had just gone in to stabilise the country so the road had been knocked about and was in a dreadful state of repair. Never, ever travel in the back of an all metal truck in such conditions, the shaking and bouncing about is traumatic and boy was I glad to arrive even though covered in dust. I was housed in a Turkish style house rented by the military. It was interesting in design in that the 1st floor landing was in the middle of the house, octagonal in shape with overhead dome lighting and furnished as a lounge. Doors all around led into bedrooms.

There were two highlights during my stay. The first one was shortly after my arrival when the restaurant/cafe in which I and several companions were having dinner came under automatic gun fire. We were not the targets specifically but rival factions were banging away at each other from opposite sides of the square and several had paused in our eating house. Bullets were whizzing and ricocheting all over the room shattering glasses and mirrors as we hurriedly crouched under our table. We had no idea what was going on but after a few minutes it stopped as suddenly as it had started. Wine had flowed during dinner so it was a case of all's well that ends well.

The second one was when I made a taxi run over the hills to Damascus in a stretched Mercedes with a family of Arabs with their women. Their spouses were dressed in black robes from head to foot with of course their faces covered so I never saw what they looked like. We stopped now and then to admire the view of the mountainous rugged terrain and at one stop I saw and heard a shepherd playing the local version of the bagpipes. These instruments I believe are played all over the world by mountain people. The Scots do not have the monopoly.

At one of the stops, about half way the Arab wives and ladies got out and performed what is known as comfort breaks with the rest of the party standing around. I was the only one embarrassed as the rest thought it was the most natural thing in the world. I reflected that there was little point in covering up their faces when this sort of thing was going on right next to the vehicle as I think I could have recognised them again from a different angle!

Damascus in Syria is a wonderful city full of ancient buildings of mosques and churches of various persuasions. It was after all the city to which St. Paul was visiting when he had his incredible experience which converted him to Christianity. I walked along the "street called straight" which was mentioned in the bible. It was at that time a covered-in, busy shopping street full of little open fronted shops. I bought a silver and zircon bracelet and observed skilled craftsmen working away making all sorts of lovely jewellery. Shops dealing with gold and silver were all open fronted and one just walked in and out at will. I just paid by my Lloyds Bank cheque which they took without question – such was Britain's standing in the glorious days of Empire. Back in Beirut in the Lebanon I had two glorious days at the St. George's hotel in the harbour where we could dive straight into deep clear blue warm sea water from the hotel quayside.

BOAC Airliner "Empyrean" 10,000feet above the Persian Gulf Tuesday 10th Oct 1944

...I feel it is all wrong my going back to India when all my instincts are to go the other way but it cannot be helped so I thought I'd have this chat with my wife, high up here and receive great comfort talking to you and Penelope....Budge darling ,I visualise there being tremendous celebrations in England when the war with Germany is finished. I think that the years of repression through black out rationing, bombs, etc will produce mass hysteria amongst celebrating crowds in the big cities and no-one can say that the people don't deserve to rejoice as it is they who have been through so much. Nevertheless, darling, to many it will be like strong drink – this mass reaction of relief I mean – so if you find yourself in parties where normal conventions are likely to break down will you please take me along with you Budge dearest, in your thoughts. – I hope you don't mind my saying this, its so hard to place ones exact thoughts on paper Budge so I hope you can see what I mean...

Headquarters Air Command. South East Asia. India 18th October '44

...Sweetheart I've had a most trying air journey from Delhi to Ceylon. I had a bit of a party with a friend of mine Terence Towell who is C.O. of the Delhi Communications flight and who used to be my assistant as Flt Cmdr in good old 159 Sqn. I met him in D and we shot around the place with one or two chaps the night before I was due to proceed to Colombo by air. Oh boy ! what a hangover I had – never will I indulge in Indian brandy again, its poison. Nevertheless I made the plane – a transport a/c with only 6 seats which were taken by senior officers. Hubb spent 10 hours all told sitting on a hard floor on the journey down here. It was most uncomfortable. I do wish transport command would have these a/c fitted up properly for passengers.

I arrived in Colombo, Ceylon at 6.30 p.m. after which I set off for H.Q. some distance away in the hills. The weather is lousy – a sticky monsoon heat. Nothing but depressing drip drip all day long in uncomfortable heat. Tomorrow I go to see an Air Cmdr on whose staff I have been earmarked to serve. If he likes the look of me then I shall be in the Air Plans section, oh dear Budge my sweet there'll be bags of work but it is bound to be interesting. I shall be working with Supremo Admiral L.L. Mountbatten's staff on planning affecting the future conduct of the Jap war !! Sounds important doesn't it but maybe when the AC has seen me I shall be posted else-where !

On the way back to the South East Asia Theatre of war I spent the Christmas period at RAF Station Habbaniyah at which was a pre-war manmade RAF base and aerodrome way out in rural countryside not far from Baghdad. I remember that of all the dates in the world to eat the ones in Iraq were by far the best. Delicious plump light brown golden colour and so full of creamy sugary taste.

The camp was virtually a small town having all the usual purpose built officers, Sgts. and Airmen's messes, work-shops and living quarters together with playing fields for all types of sport. Even a running track, tennis courts, squash courts and swimming pools. There was a hospital with nurse's quarters nearby. A cinema and theatre. A self contained area which in effect was a little bit of England. Over Christmas I went into Baghdad to a cinema and saw the Hollywood film "Gone with the Wind" which had just been released. Clark Gable and Vivien Leigh were the leading actors. (She was the wife of Sir Lawrence Olivier – Britain's No. 1 actor who was later raised to the Peerage). This film was about the American Civil War and was a classic. Many years later it was revised in colour and is still well known today over half a century later.

Return to SEAC – Staff Appointment

January 2nd 1945

...On New Year's Eve the Sturgess's took me to a very select and pleasant dinner party at the Bombay Club. It's a very pukka men's club with restricted membership. Situated in a large block of flat like buildings on the sea front overlooking the wide sweep of the bay. The party consisted of Bombay "Boxwallas" (business men) and their wives. We sat on the

roof for drinks to start with and then went into the "Ladies" room for dinner. What a dinner! Lobster and salad, turkey stuffing and ham, Christmas pudding mince pies with lots of flaming brandy crackers and the usual party hilarity.

...When the New Year was heralded in and the men were kissing their wives I retired to a dark corner of the balcony overlooking the sea and toasted your health very quietly to myself. Yes darling one I wished like hell that you could be with me and that we would be very shortly reunited. I had a huge lump in my throat as I wished you a happy New Year...

In the New Year of 1945 I returned to India to the HQ Air Command South East Asia up at Kandy in Ceylon (Sri Lanka) and had a few days off to settle in. We had quite good huts to sleep in and to preserve fruit we had wires stretched across the room from the top of the walls. From these we hung bananas, melons etc and lying in bed at night it was fun to watch rats trying to get at the fruit by a trapeze act of walking along the wire. They would get about a foot from the wall and then fall off. Then they'd try again and again until they got fed up and went off. The only other time when a rat bothered me was when I was dining in a restaurant and unseen by me a large rat was up on a beam in the ceiling who wanted a short cut to the floor. I was just raising my soupspoon to my mouth when this rat jumped down via my shoulder, down my back to the floor and sped away. Had I had a lady with me I'm sure she would have screamed her head off. It was such a quick episode that I only felt a bump and it had gone. What cheek!

The part of Ceylon we were in was high up with little knobbly peaks all around covered in palms and flowering trees. It rained every day in late afternoon so the water courses were rushing torrents when the rain sheeted down. The rest of the day it was stinking hot. Elephants were greatly prized as they were so skilled at moving heavy objects. One day I saw one ever so gently put a huge heavy safe through the open window of a newly constructed hut onto a concrete plinth inside. It was slow motion plus but it worked. It would have taken 4 men with a small crane to do the same work. One baby elephant roamed freely around our camp site and it would eat practically anything – even cigars! It was very popular and it was fascinating to see it playing games with service men.

H.Q. S.A.C. (E.P.S.) c/o Royal Air Force Ceylon

...Will you please tell Penelope that a man brought a baby elephant round to my "basher" (hut) last Friday. A little girl and so sweet she was about the size of a donkey and so playful. P. would have loved her. She "Salaamed" me by going down on her front knees and raising her trunk in the air and at the same time trumpeting. She has two weeny tusks about two inches long and is so gentle and loving. I patted her and took her trunk in my hands which she seemed to like. Someone gave her a bucket of water and after spraying it (H_2O) over herself several times she sent a jet straight through an open window slap onto a chap who was having a ziz (40 winks)!! Before she left I gave her 2 bananas which she ate in the skins and also a cigar!! Both were enjoyed equally.

Soon after settling in I was attached to Vice-Admiral Louis Mountbatten's Executive Planning Section at his HQ's in the Botanical Gardens in Peredinya. (He was the Supreme Commander in South East Asia). He himself lived in an elegant Georgian Colonial house in the gardens). His HQ was situated near his residence in one of the most beautiful part of the Gardens and as I lived outside I greatly enjoyed the drive to work every day. On the drive in to work I frequently passed an elephant who was working with his mahout (keeper) by the side of the road. He was a lucky beggar because he only worked in the morning and when I saw him again after lunch he was enjoying a bath in the cool water of a large pool off the roadside. I'm sure he recognised me as he used to wave his trunk and hoot with joy while splashing fountains of water over his body as I passed by.

Sunday13th January 1945

...I fear I shall sooner or later stir up trouble with the army staff with whom I work. The team secretary is the wife of a L/Col who holds the same post as SAC H.Q. in Ceylon. She's not in the services, a civilian. The G.1. a L/Col and G11 a major both Indian Army have their wives and they have a much better life than they would get at home. Imagine the time an unmarried Wing.Co. would have. The only difference in his pay to mine is 200 rupees (marriage allowance) There is no extra for children

Why should they cause all this misery? Why are flying personnel treated the same way as ground personnel? When they have far greater nervous worries due to their flying.

I have seen men (flying personnel and married) simply going to pieces in their last year. They cannot work, they worry about their wives and children and simply have hell until they get home. Why does the Government keep these chaps out here when they are only 50% efficient in their last year? and very unhappy.

God only knows we don't like complaining for the sake of the other ranks but I don't think the authorities realise how far reaching the effects are going to be. In my office in Ceylon we had two divorced army officers and I know one here (RAF) who divorced. Why do people make a mockery out of marriage which is the finest stabilising moral institution in the world. Hundreds of families are being wrecked right now because of this lack of foresight on the part of the govt. and Gen. Staff. And all they say is "We haven't the shipping" or "its laid down and we can't help it"

I'm afraid I've rather let loose tonight Budge but I'm sure you understand my feelings because of my great love for you …I long for my home life so lets wish and wish the days to pass quickly for April and the boat.

The Executive Planning section worked directly under the Supremo and his Chiefs of Staff of the three Services. Mountbatten and the Chiefs of Staff used to give us their outline plans and Aims for the future conduct of the advance into Burma and our syndicate of some 20-25 young battle experienced servicemen had to get down straight way and produce an overall plan with all the armed forces and logistical details worked out ready for their scrutiny. They were planning the conduct of the war in Burma some 3-6 months ahead of actual operations. It usually took us 3 to 5 days to complete these plans with a few days extra if parts had to be revised.

We worked flat out day and night to complete each stage of the advance into Burma and during the three and a half months I was there our executive planning syndicate completed plans for the retaking of Burma and the Malayan Peninsular down to and including Singapore. The RAF section, of which I was one, completed plans for the air supply of food, ammunition, petrol and oil to front line troops on the move with a fleet of Dakotas and fighters for air cover.

By then the situation was getting better and better as we already had air superiority and we were able to make it stay that way to the end. At one stage of the planning we had to send a submarine to get samples of beach sand from the island of Phuket half way down the Malayan peninsular to ascertain whether it would be possible to land tanks there as it was necessary to build an airstrip to take fighters because of their short range. (Today that Island is a favourite holiday resort in Thailand).

Saturday January 27th 1945...

I write this letter to you in a C47 (Dakota) air transport plane and we have just taken off from...(censored) you must please excuse the writing as it is a bit bumpy at the moment. Well my Sweetheart the only bit of sentiment which I shall remark on this time is that tomorrow is the 6th anniversary of our engagement day. I shall be thinking happily of you my dearest wife and of all the happiness you have brought me...

As you have read in the papers our 14th army has been going forwards into Burma by leaps and bounds and they are doing very well indeed. Their success has been due to two factors 1. Our air supply on which the army relies 2. Our air superiority over master Jap. and the consequent maximum close support the dive bombers give to the front line troops.

The battle is going so well that everybody's morale has gone up and we are all planning away like mad and becoming very excited in the process. As you will realise darling neither the Army ,Navy or RAF takes one step without it all being planned by us first !! A pat on the back, but its true. You will see startling things happen shortly which will amaze and hearten Europe because we are doing it off our own bat with no reinforcements from the European theatre.

Supremo is as pleased as punch. I have been recalled back to Ceylon to my old address as we are short of planners.

I enjoyed putting my knowledge learnt at the ME Staff College, into practical use and it was interesting and most heartening to see the team working together. I noticed that the Army and Air Force were more go-ahead than the Navy who were reluctant to take any calculated risks at all. The war had changed the attitude in the light of battle experience over the last five years with the Army and Air Force taking the brunt of initiatives against the might of the German Armed Forces with the exception of the Navy doing a splendid job of keeping Britain's lifeline open with their work of protecting conveys bringing food and supplies across the Atlantic. Our team was led by an extremely able young barrister supported by several other top class brains with high academic qualifications.

Supremo's briefing took place every morning at 0900 hrs sharp. It was held in a large warehouse inside which a stage had been built. On the hour Lord Mountbatten would walk in dressed in his white naval uniform accompanied by his chiefs of staff. All headquarters staff were present, the doors locked and guarded before proceedings began.

Everything was top secret like our own work and when Supremo gave the signal an officer from each service would give a war situation report from the raised platform which brought us bang up to date and covered the whole world on an enormous map hanging from the roof. There was one impressive American serviceman who gave the whole of the European and Pacific war state in enormous detail without a single note. It took him about ¾ hour each morning – he was a genius. All the others referred to notes.

One day this chap reported something very disturbing. The start of the Germans using the frightful V2 Ballistic missile (super rocket) on London. This information was still secret but despite this I got a message back to Budge to get out of London immediately and to stay out permanently. I couldn't give a reason as it wouldn't pass the censure. I think I used the simple code which we had arranged between us in case I was taken a prisoner of war at any time. I'm very glad I was able to warn her as shortly afterwards one landed barely a quarter of a mile away from her house in Bedford Park. These rockets went up into the stratosphere and came down without any warning.

Kandy was the ancient Capital of Ceylon and whilst there I took the opportunity to visit the Buddhist Temple of the Tooth. There is a large lake nestling in the centre of Kandy which is brimful of tortoises and the ornate temple was built centuries ago on the side of the lake. Its services are long and tedious to a westerner and consist of lots of shrill singing by groups of saffron robed young monks with the accompanying mournful notes of long low alpine-type horns being blown and the ringing of bells.

The priests were friendly and showed one around with evident pleasure as donations, especially of foreign money, helped to keep the temple in good repair. One priest showed me long thin books of 20 or so papyrus – like reeds which were the ancient records held in their library. He gave me a sample having written his name, place and the date with some writing in Sanskrit underneath. It is scribed, as it was hundreds of years ago, by means of a sharp pointed stylus which made a groove in the reed which after writing is filled in with a black powder. Today it is as good as it was 56 years ago. No wonder they were used for historical records. The date thereon is 28th March, 1945. The tooth after which the temple is named is, of course, the tooth of the Lord Buddha which is kept in the inner sanctum and only brought out on ceremonial occasions.

Occasionally my job necessitated visits to Delhi, the Rear HQ of the Armed Forces where Air Command had offices in the wonderful Secretarial building built in New Delhi in the 1930's and designed by architect Sir Edwin Lutyens.

Lutyens and Sir Herbert Baker also designed the Viceroys Palace facing East on Raisina Hill (The Palace is now the official residence of the President of India.) facing East down the Raj path (formerly Kings Way). The Secretariat buildings are positioned on either side just below the Palace and the magnificent wide tree-lined avenue stretches straight as a die past the WW1 designed Indian and British War Memorial and away into the distance.

It was in Delhi that I succumbed to heat-stroke and spent a week in sick quarters recovering from this debilitating condition. I was completely exhausted and was as weak as a kitten. I had seen this happen once before when in Egypt in 1942 when we were all having "sundowners" in the mess at Fayid on the Suez Canal our Adjutant suddenly slumped down in a chair with a ghastly ashen face drained of colour.

Sadly this varied experience in the M.E. and India/Burma came to an end when I became tour expired and received my orders to return to the UK after serving three years abroad. In retrospect I would have liked to continue to the end to witness the retaking of Singapore. To see the release of the prisoners of war and the defeat of the detested Jap army. But only if I could have had my family with me.

Overseas Leave

During my service in India I managed to get a few days leave in three famous hill stations where pre-war families went during the great heat of summer on the plains. The first one I went to was Darjeeling 7000 feet up in the Himalayas due north of Calcutta in Bengal. I stayed in the Planters Club and had a great time walking in the mountains to the snowline towards Tibet. I joined a group of servicemen on leave and we would ride on tough little sure-footed mountain ponies going hell for leather along tracks just wide enough for one pony. Sometimes these tracks had almost sheer drops of 4000 feet on one side. One stumble and you were a "goner".

The second one was up at Kashmir and Gulmarg. The latter was up at 8000 feet on the snowline. The Himalayan mountain range there had stunning scenery; so much so that Budge and I visited Gulmarg and Kashmir in 1989 on our 50th wedding anniversary we also visited Nepal and saw Everest at dawn when the sun rose.

The third one was Octacommund "Snooty Ooty" as it was called in my day. This was situated in the South Western Chats of India in beautiful high rolling country. I rented a thatch-roofed cottage from an elderly English lady and it was just like a country cottage in Devon. Chintz curtains and roses around the entrance door. I met my sister Betty's husband out there. He was on aerodrome construction with the Army Engineers. It was leopard country so I hired a car with driver and parked it by some scrub land in the shade of a tree and walked to an outcrop of rock overlooking the surrounding countryside. These big cats were known to have a kip down here having fed on a "kill". I climbed up and settled down with my water bottle and rations keeping a sharp look out for any quarry. There was plenty of evidence that leopards frequented the place from their "droppings" revealing bones of the animals they had eaten.

It was a hot day and I waited pretty nearly all day and saw nothing. Before sundown I reluctantly rejoined my vehicle only to find that my driver was locked in with all windows shut, white faced and shivering. He told me that only just before I arrived a female leopard had walked out of the bushes with her four cubs. She looked hungry and sniffed around the car with him inside. Can you beat it? There I was all day seeing nothing. There's no justice is there? One further experience I had which has no rational earthly explanation happened when I was at ACSEA in Kandy, Ceylon. It was no less than an extraordinary vivid dream I had one night. I dreamt that I was back at my parent's home in Bedford Park where I was raised and my father was leading me by the hand up the 2nd storey stairs to our third floor under the roof. He was saying – "be careful because of the rubble about" and then I noticed that the roof had been burnt off down to the top landing from above, not below. My limited knowledge of fires led me to think that fires that burn off roofs usually started below and went upwards and even in my dream I thought it strange. And though it puzzled me, I just put it down to a crazy dream and forgot about it.

At that time mail was taking up to two months to get delivered especially as we were moving about so much and it was I swear over a month after that dream that I got a letter informing me that our house in Bedford Park, West London, had been hit by an incendiarey bomb which had burnt off the roof! What was the purpose of that dream? I couldn't have alerted my family in time.

Same address

Sweetheart my first thoughts on receiving your letter about my parents house were for you, first because I am so very happy to know you are all safe, next because of our wee stock of wedding gifts and clothes. My poor darling – your splendid spirit inspires me as you have not said one word which might be interpreted as a moan. Whereas I know, being your fortunate husband that those little things given to us at the start of our happy married life meant just as much to you as mother's whole house meant to her. I do so wish I could be present by your side to comfort you…

…yes you're absolutely right Budge darling – we've had good use of our canteen and many other things too and we can easily buy these things again after the war. 'Cept my favourite Donegal tweed sports coat – remember ? Please let me know what has been destroyed. I feel very very sorry for Mother and Father Betty and Ismay – especially B who has had so much destroyed. I wrote to them immediately to ask if I could do anything to help. I told Mother a long time ago about stacking stuff in the top rooms but poor dear, she had no other place to put it, and now this has happened I wouldn't say a word about it. I expect the house is a total casualty and they will all have lost lots of stuff. …

…My darling we are fighting hard on this front and in most difficult country so please excuse if my letters arrive a little irregularly.

Return to the U.K.

C/O H.Q. BAFSEA Section 3 RAF India 16ᵗʰ January 1945

...Oh boy! Oh boy! I feel so thrilled when I think of us being able to go walking again. Penelope will always be running ahead and coming back with all sorts of things enquiring "What is it? What is this Daddy" Oh what a thrill to hear her call me Daddy

Saturday 24ᵗʰ February

...Budge have you any pointers to help me when I meet Penelope so that I don't commit any blunders which might adversely effect a little child's mind. I want to get everything just right as instinct tells me that a little girl may get very upset at something which adults may not even think about.
...be seeing you soon.

Although I was eager to get back to England and be re-united with my family, it was a wrench to leave my beloved India and all the squadrons and units I had been with for three years. I travelled to Colombo by that fantastically scenic railway journey from Kandy dropping down to the coast and was put up at the Galleface Hotel which had been taken over by the military movements section. It was right on the sea and had well kept gardens. I was assigned to a luxury cruise liner named the Strathaird, a P&O ship I think. It had been taken over by the Royal Navy as a troopship.

I had settled into a first class cabin after reporting to the Captain and being introduced to the ship's officers and I had gone up to the top deck to get some air when klaxon horns went off giving an alarm signal. Our 28,000 ton liner overlooked the harbour and roadstead leading to the entrance and the sea was full of ships of all kinds including warships. All eyes were looking some distance out and following suit I saw a ship on fire. It was a super large container ship and in no time at all it was a mass of flames from bow to stern 100 ft high. Someone said it had been torpedoed presumably by a Jap submarine. Navy boats were buzzing about to the noise of a few crumps from depth charges but it sank rapidly in a cloud of thick black smoke.

I thought this was hardly a good omen as we set sail for the Mediterranean via the Red Sea and the Suez Canal. I found myself as Wg. Cdr the senior officer amongst the troops returning home and as such everyone was incredibly nice to me in case later on they might want some favours. I did not expect any real trouble (I was only responsible for their discipline) because they were returning to England to their families having taken part in a foul war against the Japs They were also on a cruise liner with good English food and a reasonable supply of the home brews.

We had no escort because the ship was faster than a submarine but it was well armed against air attack. A fact which I noticed when we had a practise half way down the 'Med' as I had never experienced such a hail of lead being put up into the air from multiple pom-poms and the like or such a racket of noise.

The food was good with tropical fruits available but the odd thing about it was that the most popular dishes were kippers and English apples which the troops had not seen for years. I'm afraid I became quite an expert at the game of poker on the voyage which paid for alcoholic comforts. I also won a nest egg at liar dice.

Once in the 'Med' the ship increased speed and a black-out was enforced as the European war was still going on. A sharp look-out was kept and the gunners were kept up to scratch and on their toes, although of course attacks were much less likely in 1945 than in previous years. Tension increased as soon as we left Gibraltar and the 'Med' and were in the Atlantic. The war in Europe was in its last stages and the Royal Navy had largely won the battle of the Atlantic so all went well and we arrived at Greenock in Scotland on 8th May, 1945, VE day. Then by train from Glasgow to London a journey full of emotion and expectation as I saw the familiar countryside rush past. Three years away is a long time and I was longing to see Budge and small daughter Penelope. I went straight to the Savoy Hotel in the Strand where we had arranged to meet. The reception area was crowded with people but it was not long before I saw Budge and we were in each others arms. She looked radiant and Penelope now aged 4 was a real pretty picture of a happy child. We had a super lunch overlooking the Thames and life again became absolute heaven. I kidded my wife that I had arrived at reception with a large photo of her for identification! Even as a child Penelope proved she had a sound commercial sense about money when in the taxi afterwards she produced from her purse the pile of money I had left for the waiter as a tip at the Savoy.

We stayed at a well appointed small hotel close to Hyde Park and after lunch went up to Buckingham Palace and mingled with the crowds of people celebrating Victory in Europe day. Packed crowds thronged the Mall and St. James' Park as far as the eye could see. Most were in uniform and comprised Soldiers, Sailors Airmen of all the Allies in their different uniforms. I was of course in my No 1 Blue uniform.

Late afternoon outside Buck house as we called it (Buckingham Palace) we saw the King (George VI) and Queen Elizabeth (now at the time of writing the Queen Mother who has just had her 101st

birthday) and their family on the balcony of the Palace. The populace let out huge bouts of cheering as they waved acknowledgement. Everyone was milling around cheering and surging with joy at the end of European hostilities. Men and women were kissing and dancing around in joyous abandon. We got back to our hotel to find Penelope sitting up in bed being waited on by staff tempting her with delicacies as if she was royalty! The next day we returned to the Stetchworth Cottage near Newmarket in Suffolk. It was small and nicely furnished with some good antique furniture but lighting was by oil lamps and toilet facilities were non-existent except in an outside shed. Water had to be fetched from the village pump. Budge had made a snug home there ever since she had received my urgent message for her to leave London because of the V2 rockets when I was in Ceylon. She told me the sky around her had gone black with bombers, fighters and transports with gliders on 'D' day operation 'Overlord' and operation 'Market Garden' at Arnhem in Holland the year after. The reverberating noise of aero engines went on all day in both operations.

Adastral House – Staff Appointment – Air Ministry

My next posting was a staff appointment as Wing Commander at the Air Ministry in London with the Directorate of operational training. This department was responsible for the direction and facilities for the training of Army Airborne Forces, Parachute drops and gliders. Army artillery spotting aircraft pilots with Auster light aircraft and helicopter pilot training. On visits to the various units concerned I managed to do a parachute drop from 700 feet from Ringway airport (now Manchester Airport). The worst part of the short training I had was throwing myself from the top of a hangar wall without any visible means of support. All I knew was that a wire was attached to my harness which connected to an air paddle which slowed me down to the normal speed of a parachute just before I hit the ground. Ghastly to contemplate but such is the strength of the training that one just does it.

The actual drop from the Dakota aircraft was easier because you stand up in line with other Paras with your static line hooked onto an overhead cable. The door opens and there is immediately a roar of wind and engine noise and when the red light turns green the burly but cheerful Sgt gives you a slap on your shoulder and out you go one after the other. The parachute opens immediately when it reaches the end of the long static line and you find yourself looking down at the earth in peace and quiet thankful it opened. Suddenly the ground rushes up (in my case the waters of a lake) and bang I was in and going about 20 feet under water. It went dark before I struggled up to the light and surfaced panting for air. The wind caught my chute and I was dragged along for some distance before I was able to bang the release button and get rid of it. Jumping into water was necessary with short training to lessen the risk of breaking ankles or legs.

I flew an Auster which was a small light aircraft which could take off and land at slow speed in an incredibly short run. I also enjoyed rides in a helicopter which seems to defy all known forces of gravity by rising vertically when you think it should screw itself into the ground. I was also lucky to witness an Airborne Division landing exercise using gliderborne troops. I was up in the watch tower of an aerodrome in Essex and saw the sky darken with towing aircraft. The noise was terrific as these aircraft droned by and short of the aerodrome the gliders cut loose and descended in silence. Hundreds slowly came down and bang, bang, bang they landed almost in formation with a sickening crunch and out poured armed infantry some overshot and collided with trees and other gliders with the sound of splintering wood until they came to rest and spewed out the soldiers ready for action. The airfield was literally covered with gliders neatly arranged in rows. It was an amazing sight which I shall never forget.

At the end of August 1945 the United States Air Force dropped two Atomic bombs on Japan cities one on Hiroshima and the other on Nagasaki. These were new types of bombs which had been developed secretly by the United States of America and were so powerful that one single bomb destroyed a whole city. The shock was so great that Japan surrendered unconditionally a few days later and at last World War Two was over. The official date was 2nd September, 1945, when the formal surrender document was signed on the quarter deck of the battleship USS Missouri in Tokio Bay.

The relief throughout the world at war was absolute, as it was so, so sudden and the nuclear super bomb had been kept so secret. Troops all over the world were being demobilised and sent home while I was still at the Directorate of Operational Training and I had to contemplate my own future.

I reflected that I was lucky to come unscathed through six years of war despite two tours of operations over three theatres of war. In the skies over Europe, North Africa and India/Burma. I had been awarded the Distinguished Flying Cross for my operations over Germany and a second one for operations over North Africa and Burma. I also received a mention in dispatches for missions and results in the Middle East.

During the few months of 1945 whilst I was at the Directorate of operational training I had to decide on my future. After the War of course as the threat to peace had been eliminated by the defeat of the Axis powers no permanent Commissions in the Services could be given although I was offered an eight year extension of Service which would mean I would be retired at 41 years of age. Not a very good age to start a new career. So rightly or wrongly I decided to retire from the regular Air Force and was released in January, 1946 with Air Ministry granting me the right to retain rank of Wing Commander.

Post War Service

I joined Royal Auxiliary Air Force in 1949 and was commissioned in the Fighter Control Branch of the new reconstituted Royal Air Force on extended service on the active list as Commanding Officer of 3609 West Riding Fighter Control Unit at Yeadon which is now Leeds Bradford Civilian Airport.

I developed this unit for five years from scratch. The R. Aux. Air Force is run on the lines of the Territorial Army. Its members were recruited from the civilian population and training took place at weekends and on active service fortnights each year. We trained controllers on mobile radar units who directed our fighter aircraft on to incoming enemy aircraft whilst watching their movements on the radar screens. We also trained considerable numbers of young women who manned the secret underground control centres responsible for the air sector in the UK or elsewhere. During the five years we were able to take part in NATO exercises at regular RAF Radar Centres around the coast of Britain and on one occasion in Germany at Wildenrath under war conditions. These exercises simulated an attack using even more powerful atomic nuclear bombs when the war was envisaged only to last 3 days as all the cities on both sides would be pulverised. The safest place at that time would have been underground in the RAF!

After commanding the Fighter Control Unit for five years I was transferred to the Reserve of Officers Ground Branch and finally completed my Service career on 19th November, 1959.

4.   Post-War ~ 1946-2001

After leaving the regular service I took a Master Printers Course at the London School of Printing and joined the family firm of Beck and Inchbold of Leeds and London. After my father died in 1948 I was appointed Managing Director. It was a medium-sized firm of some 120 employees, housed in an old-fashioned five-storey building in the centre of Leeds. During the 20 years until 1968 I developed the firm's potential by selling the old premises and building a new factory on a two-acre site on a small Industrial Estate at Seacroft, on the outskirts of the city. To the letterpress and lithographic processes we already had, I added the new screen print process. The new factory had a clear span of 120 feet and production was organised on a flowline principle. The effort after taking over after the war when everything was run down and all new machinery was exported and the planning and moving to a new factory gave me the businessman's complaint – a duodenal ulcer – which resulted in an operation. In 1967 I sold the company to the Westminster Press, part of the S. Pearson Group, owned by Lord Cowdray's family, and retired to Jersey.

There I became bored and depressed, having nothing to do, and at the age of 55, when I was still pretty active, having recovered after three years from the ulcer operation, I co-founded the Estate Agency of *Beck & Deane* and thoroughly enjoyed helping to build it up from scratch to become one of the principle property firms on the island of Jersey, before retiring finally in 1983, aged 70.

As I write it is now the year 2001 and looking back on a long life full of variety and excitement and no small amount of danger I feel that I contributed my bit satisfactorily to the Allied victory over the Axis Powers during the six long years of World War II and to the wellbeing of Britain's postwar era in helping its exports and general commerce through the "art preservative of all arts" – i.e. the printing industry – which provided the oil for the smooth running of industry in general.

Although life is full of ups and downs, successes and disappointments, I feel I was blessed with a happy marriage and a loyal family to see me through all the traumas of life and the joy of having grandchildren and even a great-grandchild and to witness them growing up and choosing and developing their own careers in a very different world to mine.

Obituaries ~ January 2003

Wing Commander J. Leighton Beck

Airman who destroyed 250,000 gallons of German petrol at Tobruk and went on to direct airstrikes against the Japanese

In a wartime career of almost constant action, J. Leighton Beck served in most of the major air theatres, both as a pilot and air commander and on the staff, directing tactical air operations. He completed two tours flying bombers, the first over Germany in the early days of the war, as the twin-engined aircraft of Bomber Command – in Beck's case Wellingtons – strove to make some impression on the output of German industry, suffering frightful losses as they did so.

He won a DFC for this, as he did on his next tour of operations, which was split between the Middle East and the India-Burma theatre. In the spring of 1942 the squadron of Liberators of which he was a flight commander was intended for the Far East, where the Japanese were triumphant and the air situation was desperate.

But when it arrived in Egypt, en route for India, it was ordered to remain there and throw its weight into a campaign which, too, was going badly. Rommel was driving the British Eighth Army steadily back and a fierce struggle for air superiority was raging. The four-engined Liberator with its heavy bomb load and long range added significant punch to the RAF in the Middle East, and by autumn 1942 had inflicted great damage on Afrika Corps supply lines.

With the Middle East crisis surmounted, the squadron continued to India where it flew sorties against the Japanese from bases
in Bengal. Beck remained in India after the end of his second tour,
and after commanding RAF Poona had what he always regarded as
the most interesting posting of his career, that of bombing
operations adviser to the 3rd Tactical Air Force at Imphal. As such
he played a major role in directing air strikes on Japanese positions
in the campaign which was the turning point of the war in the
India-Burma theatre.

John Leighton Beck was born in Chiswick in 1920 and educated
at Ardingly College, Haywards Heath. He trained as an estate
agent, valuer and surveyor, but in 1935, while working for his
chartered surveyor's exam, was attracted by a newspaper
advertisement for short service commission RAF officers.

Beck never did take his qualification. He was commissioned
into the RAF in 1936, and in 1937 went out to Egypt to a squadron
of Vickers Valentia biplane bomber/troop carriers, based at
Heliopolis. Later in the year he was posted to 99 Squadron at
Mildenhall, equipped with the Handley Page Heyford, the last of
the RAF's biplane heavy bombers and a ponderous anachronism in
an era when the Luftwaffe already had squadrons of fast mono-
plane machines.

Late in 1938 the squadron at last received the Barnes Wallis-
designed Wellington. In this it took part in the summer of 1939 in
what was meant to be a demonstration to the German high
command of the RAF's capacity to hit at Berlin and other distant
German cities. A non-stop flight by several squadrons from
Mildenhall to Paris and thence to Marseilles and return was given
a good deal of publicity in the French and British press – but had
no noticeable effect on Hitler's war plans.

When war broke out the Wellington squadrons practised painstaking close formation flying, in the belief that their defensive armament could repel any fighter attack. In October 1939 Beck was posted to a specialist navigation course at St Athan, South Wales, and was not with the squadron on the raid during which this comfortable theory was cruelly exposed.

On December 14, 1939, on an "armed reconnaissance" of German shipping in the Schillig Roads, 99 Squadron attempted to shoot it out with the Me109s which intercepted it. Five of 12 Wellingtons were shot down and a sixth crashed on the way home. The loss of so many mess-mates profoundly affected Beck, who was under no illusion what his own chances of survival would have been, had he been been there.

In February 1940, Beck was posted to 214 Squadron, and when the Phoney War (during which Chamberlain's Government had forbidden the bombing of Germany) ended abruptly in May of that year, was involved in raids on the Ruhr and further afield to Magdeburg, Berlin and Stettin (now Szczecin). One of his most successful sorties was an attack on a large Berlin gas producing plant, which he severely damaged. Beck was later asked by the BBC to do a broadcast on the raid, which is described in Ivor Halstead's wartime book Wings of Victory. Beck was awarded his first DFC in November 1940.

After a spell at Bomber Command HQ, in March 1942 he was posted to 159 Squadron, which had just received the powerful American-built B24 Liberator. After a period testing the aircraft's capabilities on ocean sorties for Coastal Command, the squadron was sent to India.

The first staging post was Gibraltar, and Beck was entrusted with assessing whether or not the Liberator could actually get down on the Rock's short runway, before the rest of the squadron was committed. Half Gibraltar turned out to witness the first landing there of a four-engined bomber, since the tailfins of Wellingtons that had overshot, sticking out of the sea at the end of the runway, attested to the difficulty of the enterprise. By approaching at just above stalling speed and cutting the throttles right back just before the wheels touched the runway, Beck was able to pull up with ten yards to spare.

Thereafter, from their base on the Suez Canal the Liberators of 159 Squadron carried out attacks on shipping and Axis-occupied Libyan ports by day and night, also ranging as far afield as the Italian naval base at Taranto. As Rommel advanced to Alamein the squadron had to withdraw to bases in Palestine from where Beck carried out his most successful attack, a direct hit on a German fuel dump at Tobruk, which destroyed 250,000 gallons of petrol desperately needed for the Afrika Korps' panzers. He was mentioned in dispatches.

Besides his courage and skill in the air, Beck was well liked by the squadron's ground crews. In Palestine many of these were Australians who serviced the aircraft in stifling heat and lived in the open under canvas. These men hotly resented the insistence on maintaining standards of dress at all times beloved of some of the sticklers for discipline among squadron and station command-ers. On one occasion the intercession of Beck with his superior officer almost certainly headed off a mutiny.

In November 1942, with Rommel in retreat after Alamein, the squadron carried on to India. There, from bases in Bengal it attacked Japanese airfields, supply dumps and troop concentra-tions in Burma. It was perilous work conducting operations over the inhospitable terrain of the Chin and Naga mountain ranges, with the ever present danger of Japanese fighters, and forced landings largely out of the question for damaged aircraft in the dense teak forests. At the end of the tour Beck was awarded a Bar to his DFC.

He was next given command of RAF Poona, 1,000 miles to the west in the Deccan. Among his duties was to liaise with the local community, which on one occasion included helping to dispose of a rogue leopard that was terrorising a hill village and had killed several young girls as they drew water from the well. Two rounds from Beck's Lee Enfield eventually put paid to the beast, after it leapt out at a tracking party from tree cover and savaged the local chief of police who had organised the hunt for it.

In December 1943, Beck was posted to the headquarters of 221 group, 3rd Tactical Air Force, calling in airstrikes to support IV Corps in General Slim's 14th Army. With its Hurribombers (Hurricanes adapted for ground attack), Spitfires and a fleet of troop-carrying Dakotas, the 3rd TAF played a decisive role in the defence of Imphal, supplying it by air throughout a desperate two-and-a-half-month siege. He next went to Mountbatten's South-East Asia Command staff, planning for the retaking of Burma and Malaya. He ended his wartime service in the Air Ministry, planning parachute and glider pilot training, finally being demobilised in 1946.

After training at the London School of Printing, he joined the family printing firm, Beck & Inchbold, in Leeds, becoming managing director and then chairman. In 1967, after suffering from a duodenal ulcer which required urgent surgery, he sold the company to Westminster Press and retired to Jersey. However, at only 55, he then founded a firm of estate agents, Beck and Deane, building it to a leading position among property firms on the island. He finally retired in 1983.

Beck is survived by his wife, Budge, whom he married in 1939, and by two daughters.

Wing Commander J. Leighton Beck, DFC and Bar, wartime bomber pilot, was born in London on November 15, 1912. He died in Jersey on January 2, 2003, aged 90.

© *The Times*, London, January 20, 2003.

Flying Ace and founder of estate agency

WING COMMANDER John Leighton Beck, who has died at the age of 90, was an RAF officer who, in the Second World War, was an exceptional Flight Commander and formation leader. In his retirement years, he was co-founder of the Jersey estate agency, Beck and Dean.

While serving in the Middle East in 1943, he led repeated daylight raids on Afrika Korps supply lines, in the face of intense opposition from anti-aircraft fire and enemy fighters.

On a daylight bomber raid on Tobruk in June 1942, while leading a formation of six Liberator aircraft from his own 159 Squadron, he managed to achieve a direct hit on the major fuel dump of Rommel's Afrika Korps, totally destroying it and 250,000 gallons of fuel. This was at a time when petrol supplies were of vital importance to Rommel. The raid was one of the most successful in a six-month bombing campaign. By September 1943 Rommel only had enough petrol for his tanks and vehicles to travel 60 miles, and only half his supplies were reaching him before the Battle of El Alamein.

For his service in the Middle East, he received a bar to the Distinguished Flying Cross and was mentioned in dispatches.

He had received the DFC three years earlier in August 1940 for a bombing raid on Berlin. On that occasion, in the face of heavy anti-aircraft fire, he made a successful attack on a gas works, causing considerable destruction and starting a great number of fires.

In the citation it was said: 'By his devotion to duty and excellent navigation, he has consistently set a most admirable and praiseworthy example.' He received the DFC from the hands of King George VI in November 1940.

In his unpublished autobiography, Chocks Away, he wrote: 'War in the air is a matter of luck and circumstance. The odds are much loaded against your survival.

'People have asked me if I felt fear on these occasions, and my answer is no. Apprehension and anxiety: yes (in plenty), but fear—no.

'In the middle of the onslaught by fighters, when I saw chunks of metal coming off my engines, the only feeling I had was as if an extremely sharp knife was being drawn slowly across my throat, just cutting the skin.'

Wing Commander John Leighton Beck, DFC and Bar, who was known familiarly by his middle name, was born in Bedford Park, west London, in November 1912.

He was educated at Colet Court preparatory school in Hammersmith and then at Ardingly College, Sussex, where he excelled at ball games and was a first-class shot, captaining the shooting eight for two years.

On leaving school he trained as a surveyor before joining the RAF in 1936 and was awarded his 'Wings' early in 1937. He was posted with 216 Squadron in Egypt, and then to 99 Squadron at Mildenhall, a squadron which the following year was re equipped with Wellington bombers.

The first months of the war were spent on a specialist navigational course and in February 1940 he joined 214 Squadron, in which he served until March 1941.

He took part in one of the first raids on Berlin, later making a BBC broadcast about the experience. At the end of his tour he had lost most of his friends, who had been either killed or captured.

On promotion to Squadron Leader, he was posted to Headquarters Bomber Command, where he remained for 14 months until posted to the newly formed 159 Squadron to fly American B24 four-engine bomber aircraft, known in the RAF as Liberators.

He moved with his squadron in May 1942 to Egypt via Gibraltar. The destination was to have been India, but the squadron was diverted to become part of the allied strategic Air Force ordered to prevent food, armaments.

petrol and oil reaching Rommel's advancing army and to attack enemy troop concentrations in the desert.

For the next six months his squadron operated in this theatre of war by night and by day, attacking targets as far afield as Italy and Crete, first from Egypt and then from Palestine.

The squadron moved on to India in November 1942, where from Bengal they operated against Japanese targets in Burma. In June 1943 he was promoted to Wing Commander and posted as station commander to RAF Poona, a base that was being developed as a transit and training pool for air-crew arriving from the UK.

Six months later he was posted to the staff of the Third Tactical Air Force at Imphal, near the Burmese border, as a bombing operations adviser. The force was in support of the 14th Army, which had been defeated in Burma and was, at that time, preparing to take on the Japanese forces that were poised to attack India through Imphal.

He was based there while Imphal was cut off (except by air) by Japanese forces. The 14th Army, which had been given the order to fight until the last man, contained and defeated the big push to re-capture Burma. Wing Commander Beck was an observer in the thick of the fighting, calling up air support to bomb Japanese positions.

After the conclusion of the Siege of Imphal, he attended the Army and Air Force Staff College in Palestine, before returning to Headquarters Air Command South East Asia in Ceylon. There he was attached to Vice-Admiral Louis Mountbatten (the supreme commander in South East Asia), as part of the executive planning section producing an overall plan for the conduct of the war in Burma.

On completion of his three-year overseas tour he returned to the UK, arriving back just in time for VE Day. His next posting was at the Air Ministry. He retired from the RAF in 1946, but joined the Royal Auxiliary Air Force in 1949. He completed his service career in 1959, commanding 3609 Fighter Control Unit at Yeadon, Leeds.

After leaving the regular service, he took a master printer's course at the London School of Printing and joined the family company of Beck and Inchbold, of Leeds and London, of which he became managing director after his father's death in 1948. For the next 20 years he developed the firm's potential by selling the company's old building in central Leeds and building a new factory on the town's outskirts.

Following an operation for a duodenal ulcer, he sold the company to the Westminster Press and retired to Jersey, aged 55. Being, in his own words, 'bored and depressed', he co-founded the Beck and Dean estate agency, which became one of the Island's principal property firms. He retired finally in 1983 at the age of 70.

In Jersey he was president of the Kart and Motor Club for five years and president of the Past Rotarians Club (1979) and Probus Club (1982).

A man of wide interests, he enjoyed many sports and has been described as someone who had a sense of decency, integrity, a strong sense of humour and a great ability to make spontaneous friendships.

Wing Commander Beck is survived by his wife, Mary (née Broad), always known as 'Budge and by his daughters Penelope and Priscilla ('Scilla), and their families, to whom the JEP extends its sympathy.

© *The Jersey Evening Post*

Wing Commander John Beck

Wing Commander John Beck, who has died aged 90, survived long periods of sustained bomber operations over Europe and North Africa before being posted to provide air support for Major-General Orde Wingate's Chindits behind enemy lines in Burma; the experience of meeting the eccentric soldier made him decide to experience for himself jungle operations on the ground.

Beck had arrived in late 1943 at Imphal to see flashes and smoke erupting on the airstrip about half a mile away, followed by noisy crumps. "I thought here I was, an RAF pilot, experiencing what it was like being in the Army against a hardened and disciplined and ruthless enemy. I have to say I really enjoyed it.

"The order of no retreat gave a real buzz. Morale was high, and the RAF were at last achieving air superiority over the Japanese Air Force. It was heaven to be cut off from Group HQ as the paperwork dwindled to practically nothing."

Beck's job of briefing fighter-bomber and transport units from a mud hut while Imphal was being harassed by the Japanese 15th Army left him in no doubt about the precariousness of the position. But even though he was a staff officer, and not an operational commander, Beck made a point of accompanying the troops into action, carrying his revolver and sten gun. This enabled him both to check the effectiveness of RAF forward radio control parties and to call for Hurricane fighter-bombers to soften up bunker complexes.

The bravery and dedication of the soldiers, as well as the battle cries of Indian and Gurkha battle formations attacking the Japanese in their bunkers, left him spellbound, he remembered.

Beck accompanied 63 Brigade as it moved out of Imphal to check the advancing Japanese 33rd division. As he moved forward with his sergeant wireless operator and two mules laden with their bulky equipment, he was astonished by how flexibly he was adapting to jungle warfare.

When the brigade was ordered to take an enemy hilltop bunker, Beck called up a squadron of Hurri-bombers to soften it up; finally, after bitter hand-to-hand fighting, the position fell; two 75mm guns and one disease-ridden surviving Japanese were captured.

Having satisfied himself that the RAF's forward control worked, Beck returned to a severely battered Imphal then went on to a staff college course at Haifa in Palestine.

John Leighton Beck was born on November 15 1912 at Bedford Park, west London. He was educated at Ardingly College, and won The Daily Telegraph sharpshooting competition at Bisley.

He trained as an estate agent with Ferris and Puckridge, then moved on to Debenham, Tewson & Chinnock. It was while updating the Ordnance Survey map at the Isle of Sheppey in Kent that he noticed a target-towing biplane. This aroused an interest in flying and, after paying five shillings for a joyride at an air display, he answered an advertisement offering short service commissions for pilots.

Beck was commissioned in 1936, and the following year joined No 216, a bomber-transport squadron equipped with obsolescent Vickers Valentias at Heliopolis in Egypt.

Towards the end of the year Beck returned to No 99 Squadron, which switched from Handley Page Heyford biplane bombers to Vickers Wellingtons, at Mildenhall, Suffolk. Two days before the outbreak of war Beck was surprised to be ordered with the squadron to Newmarket racecourse to operate from the Rowley Mile gallops.

Operations were planned in the jockeys' weighing-in room, and most personnel slept in the grandstand. One of Beck's earliest trips was to show the flag by passing low over the Arc de Triomphe.

When, in February 1940, he was posted to No 214 Squadron, Beck began a long run of operations against targets in Germany and the barges preparing to invade Britain from French ports. Sometimes he handed over to his second pilot while he occupied the bomb aimer's position in the front turret.

On one sortie, Beck braved a balloon barrage to press home his attack at low level despite his aircraft being damaged by a cable. On another a piece of red-hot shrapnel was embedded in the parachute cushioning his seat. In November 1940 his completion of a strenuous tour of some 30 operations was recognised with a DFC.

Early in the New Year Beck was "rested" in the navigation section at Bomber Command, while being enrolled in the local defence unit, jocularly known as the Southdown Rifles.

After a year he resumed operations as a flight commander with No 159, a newly formed four-engine Liberator squadron which was dispatched to Egypt. Six months of unremitting attacks on enemy-held positions in Libya followed. Beck's Liberator was hit repeatedly; he once returned from a raid on Tobruk to find that a bullet from a German night fighter had passed through the length of the sole of the mid-upper gunner's shoe.

Recalling a Benghazi raid, Beck noted: "We were attacked by three fighters. We got a terrible hammering. I could hear bullets and cannon shells smashing their way down the fuselage, one or two hitting the armour plating behind my back . . . and see pieces of a port engine being shot off."

Then a starboard engine caught fire, and Beck went into a screaming dive which extinguished the blaze in time for him to pull up over the sea.

In November 1942, Beck was ordered with No 159 to India, where he learned that his desert exploits had been recognised with a Bar to his DFC and a mention in dispatches. However, there was no respite as he targeted Japanese fuel dumps, supplies, bridges and railway yards in Burma; the monsoon conditions took a greater toll than operations until the squadron was reduced to three serviceable aircraft.

After completing his second tour of operations Beck was rested as station commander at Poona, where he was asked to assist in the hunt for a rogue leopard which had been terrorising villagers in the hills to the south. When the animal broke cover a police officer opened fire.

"The leopard roared and in three enormous bounds was on top of a policeman," Beck recalled. "As the animal made off into some trees I fired my .303 service rifle. I put two rounds into him."

The leopard was found dead under a bush; the policeman was severely wounded in the throat and shoulder. Afterwards the local headman was full of fervent thanks as the animal had carried off and killed several young women who were drawing water from the village well.

By June 1945, Beck's paper-pushing abilities had been honed at Air Command South-East Asia and the Haifa staff college. He returned home to work at the Air Ministry's operational directorate until 1946.

Following a brief spell in the Civil Aviation ministry's training branch, Beck studied for a year at the London School of Printing before joining the family printing firm, Beck & Inchbold, where he later became chairman and managing director.

He also bought and developed a screen printing company and, after 20 years, amalgamated his business interest with the Westminster Press when, in 1968, he moved to Jersey. Meanwhile, he had retained his association with the RAF, serving in the Royal Auxiliary Air Force until 1959.

In 1973, Beck co-founded Beck and Deane as estate agents on the island, running the business until he finally retired in 1983.

He was sometime president of the Jersey Kart and Motor Club, enjoying golf at the La Moye and membership of the Royal Channel Islands Sailing Club and the St Saviours Bowling Club.

Beck, who died on January 2, married, in 1939, Mary Irene Broad, known as Budge. They had two daughters.

© The Daily Telegraph

Citations for DFC and Bar

BECK, John Leighton, F/L (37785, Royal Air Force) – No.214 Squadron – Distinguished Flying Cross – awarded as per *London Gazette* dated 22 November 1940. Public Record Office Air 2/8351 has the recommendation, of which the following digested text was the citation sent to Air Ministry Awards Committee:

> "Since June 1940, this officer has carried out 20 raids over Germany and enemy occupied territory. On the night of August 30th, 1940, he made a successful bombing attack in the face of heavy anti-aircraft fire, on a coal gas works near Berlin, causing considerable destruction and fires. On another occasion, this officer in spite of the presence of a balloon barrage, descended to a low level and delivered an attack which he pressed home. His aircraft came in collision with a balloon cable, which was successfully severed. Flight Lieutenant Beck has displayed excellent powers of navigation, great devotion to duty and exceptional dash and determination."

The following citation for the Bar to DFC was published in *Flight*, 29 July 1943:

> "Squadron Leader Beck has repeatedly led formations of aircraft many hundreds of miles over enemy territory in daylight and pressed home his attacks in the face of intense enemy opposition. On one occasion he was instrumental in destroying a very large quantity of petrol in tanks at a time when such supplies were of vital importance to the enemy."

RECORD OF SERVICE

OF

WING COMMANDER JOHN LEIGHTON BECK DFC*(37785)

DATE AND PLACE OF BIRTH: 15 November 1912, Acton

APPOINTMENTS AND PROMOTIONS

Granted short service commission as Acting Pilot Officer on probation in the General Branch of the Royal Air Force	4 May 36
Graded as Pilot Cfficer on probation	24 Apr 37
Confirmed in appointment	27 Aug 37
Flying Officer	24 Dec 38
Transferred to the Reserve of Air Force Officers and retained on Active List	9 Mar 40
Flight Lieutenant	3 Sep 40
Acting Flight Lieutenant	14 Sep 40
Acting Squadron Leader	5 Mar 41
Squadron Leader (Temporary)	1 Dec 41
Acting Wing Commander	6 Jun 43
Squadron Leader (war substantive)	6 Sep 43
Wing Commander (Temporary)	1 Jul 44
Last day of service	3 Apr 46
Relinquished commission and retains rank of Wing Commander	19 Nov 49
Commissioned as a Squadron Leader in the Fighter Control Branch of the reconstituted Royal Air Force	19 Nov 49
Acting Wing Commander	1 Aug 53
Service extended on the Active List as Commanding Officer of 3609 West Riding Fighter Control Unit until 8 Jan 55	19 Nov 54
Relinquished appointment as Commanding Officer of 3609 West Riding Fighter Control Unit	
Transferred to the Reserve	9 Jan 55
Transferred to the Ground Branch (Ground Section)	3 Feb 55
Relinquished commission on completion of service	19 Nov 59

POSTINGS

Civil Flying School Hanworth	9 Mar 36
Depot Uxbridge	4 May 36
No 8 Flying Training School Montrose	16 May 36
No 216 (Bomber Training) Squadron Middle East	27 May 37
No 1 Depot Uxbridge	30 Oct 37
No 99 (B) Squadron Mildenhall	5 Dec 37
School of Air Navigation St Athan Manston.	11 Apr 39
No 99 Squadron Mildenhall	13 May 39
School of Air Navigation St Athan	9 Oct 39
No 99 Squadron Mildenhall	5 Feb 40

1

~ 169 ~

```
No 214 Squadron Stradishall                                    13 Feb 40
Stradishall                                                    14 Sep 40
Headquarters Bomber Command High Wycombe                       26 Feb 41
No 1653 Conversion Unit Bomber Command                         30 Mar 42
Polebrook Bomber Command                                       27 Apr 42
Middle East (Pool)                                              4 Jun 42
Wastage Pool India                                              2 Nov 42
No 159 Squadron India                                           4 Nov 42
Station Headquarters Poona India                                6 Jun 43
Air Transit Pool Poona India                                   17 Jun 43
Poona India                                                    11 Nov 43
No 221 Group Allied Command South East Asia       RAF/ARMY.S.C.          27 Dec 43
3rd Tactical Air Force Allied South East Asia   3 months Staff College.Haifa  13 May 44
Headquarters Air Command South East Asia          Palestine. ME.          19 Jun 44
No 1 Personnel Despatch Centre                                  5 Apr 45
Air Ministry Directorate of Operational Training               13 Jun 45
No 100 Personnel Despatches Centre                              2 Jan 46
Released
No 3609 West Riding Fighter Control Unit                       19 Nov 49
No 7134 Reserve Flight                                          1 Feb 56
No 7268 Reserve Flight                                          5 Oct 56
No 7274 Reserve Flight                                          3 Dec 56
```

HONOURS AND AWARDS

```
Distinguished Flying Cross London Gazetted                     22 Nov 40
Mentioned in Despatches London Gazetted                         1 Jan 43
Bar to Distinguished Flying Cross London Gazetted              18 Jun 43
```

MEDALS

```
1939/45 Star
Africa Star and Clasp
Aircrew Europe Star
Burma Star
Defence Medal
War Medal 1939/45
Elizth II Coronation medal.
```

S C RAFTREE
for Air Secretary

2